CONCEPTS
OF
THE
UNIVERSE

CONCEPTS
OF
THE
UNIVERSE

PAUL W. HODGE

DEPARTMENT OF ASTRONOMY
UNIVERSITY OF WASHINGTON

McGRAW-HILL BOOK COMPANY

NEW YORK   SYDNEY
ST. LOUIS   TORONTO
SAN FRANCISCO   MEXICO
LONDON   PANAMA

**CONCEPTS
OF
THE
UNIVERSE**

Library of Congress Catalog Card Number 69-18715

2 3 4 5 6 7 8 9 O V B V B 7 6 5 4 3 2 1 0

PREFACE

The universe is a pretty big place and this is only a small book. I have tried to compensate for this inequity as much as possible by using pictures. Photographs, drawings, and charts sometimes make obscure ideas seem reasonable (even when they aren't), and without a clear mental picture of some of the features of our universe it is impossible to grasp the concepts of cosmology.

The book assumes nothing on the part of the reader except the ability to read. It requires no mathematics and no prior astronomical knowledge, and the technical terms used are defined as they come up. Thus, whether it is read as a text in a physical science course, as a supplement to an astronomy course, or as no more than fun, it can be used at any time, without regard to curriculum or background. The book has one goal: to give a brief and simple account of science's biggest problem—discovering the properties of the universe as a whole.

Paul W. Hodge

CONTENTS

PHOTOGRAPH CREDITS

CONCEPTS
OF
THE
UNIVERSE

CHAPTER 1

WHAT IS THE UNIVERSE?

The word "universe" means different things to different people. It means one thing to the scientist and often quite a different thing to others. For instance, Bostonians who call their city the *Hub of the Universe* are using the term to refer to what others call *New England;* and the judges of the Miss Universe contest use the term to refer only to those countries on the earth that send in contestants. The Bostonian does not mean to imply that Boston is vital to the economy of the scientists' universe, or even to the economy of the local Galaxy. And, if a little green maiden from some other planetary system entered the Miss Universe contest, the judges might be hard-pressed to use their usual criteria and might prefer to disqualify her on the grounds that she comes from outside the universe, as they define it. It cannot be said that our colloquial use of the word "universe" is universal.

Astronomers define the word "universe" in three different ways. One definition means all that we can see. This is the *observable universe,* including all the stars and distant galaxies that can be detected directly by the reception of radiation emitted by them. The observable universe is the astronomer's laboratory, where he explores, where he checks out hypotheses and ideas, and where he gathers data to enable him to formulate new ideas about the nature

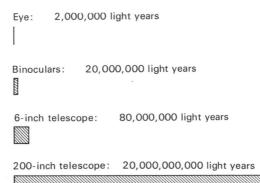

Eye: 2,000,000 light years

Binoculars: 20,000,000 light years

6-inch telescope: 80,000,000 light years

200-inch telescope: 20,000,000,000 light years

Figure 1   The size of the observable universe as seen by the eye and by telescopes of various sizes.

of what he sees. The observable universe is continually growing as new and more powerful receiving equipment is developed for the astronomer's use.

The second definition means all that we can see plus everything else. This is the *entire universe,* which has to be treated mathematically, metaphysically, or philosophically by extrapolation from what we know about the observable universe. We don't even know whether there *is* such a thing as an entire universe.

The third definition means that part of the entire universe that is described by the laws of physics as we know them. This is the *physical universe,* which is a slight extension of the observable universe since it includes things that cannot be seen but that are detected by their effects on things we do see. Because we do not yet live in an entirely scientific world, there are things that are not yet treated by the scientific method, and this third definition excludes those parts of reality. The physical universe refers to the part of the universe that can be treated in a scientific way.

Cosmology is the study of the physical universe. The biggest problem facing astronomy today is the cosmological question—the nature of the universe—and it is the one problem that people are working on now that is least likely to find a solution in the next few years. Almost everyone in science believes that he is on the verge of solving the problem he is working on, but it is a rare cosmologist who believes that he will solve the problem of cosmology once and for all in the near future, or even in his lifetime. Nevertheless, the problem is being attacked with tremendous vigor because of a large number of very exciting discoveries that have taken place in the last few years.

One of the key questions in cosmology is whether or not the universe is bounded: does it have an edge, or border, where it stops?

There are various ways that we examine this question. In the first place, the observable universe is bounded by the limits of our equipment. This boundary, of course, is not a permanent one because every year we're working out new methods of improving telescopes and other astronomical instruments. In fact, the largest optical telescope in the world, the 200-inch telescope on Palomar Mountain, is an instrument that was designed especially for the purpose of exploring the most distant realms of space in hope of answering the cosmological question. The limits of observation are

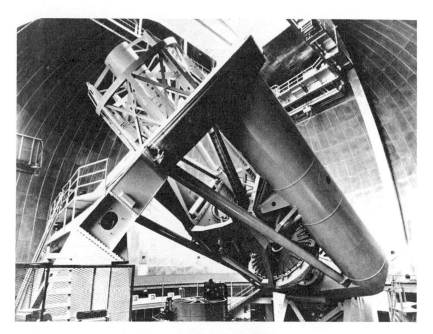

Figure 2　The 200-inch telescope at Palomar Mountain.

Figure 3   A remote observatory in the Australian mountains near Coona-
barabran.

Figure 4 The 300-foot radio telescope of the National Radio Astronomical Observatory in West Virginia.

Figure 5 A galaxy (NGC 2655) with large amounts of dust, showing the way in which dust obscures more-distant stars.

being extended by other kinds of techniques, particularly radio telescopes, and every time more knowledge is added about the most-
distant objects we can see, more-distant ones are found, one way or
another. The universe tends to grow insofar as the observable
boundary is concerned. Recently, it has doubled in size every five or
so years.

What about the actual boundaries of the universe? If you look with
larger and larger telescopes in a particular direction, will you ever
see the end of the universe? First, there is a possible physical limit
that might occur. We know that there is a lot of matter in the universe, much of it in the form of stars, but possibly even more in the
form of gas and dust. We can conceive that, if we look to tremendously large distances, the dust would eventually obscure what we
see, until finally we would be looking at just blankness where the
total amount of dust we are looking through has obscured everything

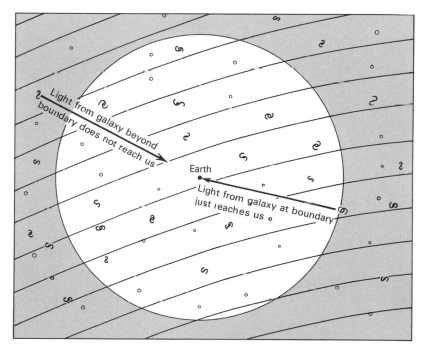

Figure 6   A dusty universe that has a dust boundary beyond which light
does not reach us.

beyond it. This is a little different from the boundaries of the observable universe because, once we come to that (if such a limit exists), no matter how big our telescope is we won't have any chance of seeing anything farther out.

At the moment we haven't reached anything like such a boundary because, as we go farther and farther, we find that the obscuration of these distant objects is really very small. There apparently is not as much dust as would be necessary to cause obscuration to be an important limitation to us as yet.

Another boundary, the "velocity boundary," is much more serious. The most-distant objects that we see in the universe have high velocities because the universe itself is expanding, continuously growing in size. We find, as we go farther and farther away, that galaxies have higher and higher velocities away from us, and recently we've encountered velocities that are very nearly the speed

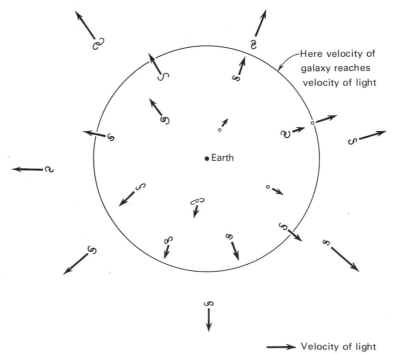

Figure 7 A universe with a velocity boundary. This universe does not obey the laws of relativity.

of light. Since the only communication we have with these distant galaxies is their light, the only way we can detect them is by the light coming from them. There is going to be a rather awkward situation when we find a galaxy so far away that its velocity *is* the velocity of light. It will be going away so fast that any light it sends in our direction will never quite get here. Thus, if this trend of higher and higher velocities continues (and it may not), we will eventually reach the point where galaxies will disappear. We'll just see blank sky at that distance and the observable universe will have been completely probed by our instruments, even though there may be millions of galaxies beyond that. There are mathematical models of the universe that have galaxies beyond that "disappearing" distance, going even faster than the velocity of light. Of course the laws of relativity forbid this, and such models are of only academic interest.

These are observable boundaries imposed by the nature of matter and by our ability. One boundary is caused by the smallness of our telescopes, the second is caused by obscuration (which probably won't turn out to be important), and the third is caused by the velocity of the objects. There is also a very different kind of boundary that is not a human or physical limitation but a geometrical one. It is possible that the universe is bounded by geometry alone. One way of looking at the universe—and this is Newton's way—is to consider that it is infinite and has no boundary. This means that, in the entire universe, the true physical universe is an infinitely large thing with no edges. If this is indeed the case, then we don't worry about true boundaries because the only boundaries are those imposed by ourselves. However, there are difficulties with this view since there are observations which do not seem to agree with the predictions that can be made from the newtonian hypothesis of an infinite universe. For instance, latest measurements indicate that the most-distant galaxies have velocities inconsistent with a newtonian type of infinite universe.

One can avoid this difficulty by hypothesizing that the universe is not shaped the way one's intuition tells him it must be, a suggestion that comes from some work of Lobachevsky, a Russian mathematician. Lobachevsky showed that, if one didn't accept Euclid's axiom about parallel lines (two straight lines that are parallel to each other will extend to infinity and never intersect, always remaining at the same distance), then one could put in a much looser law about parallel lines that allows them to diverge or converge. This gives a whole new system of geometry that is perfectly self-consistent and logical.

Einstein found that, by using such a noneuclidean geometry, he could work out a cosmology of the universe such that the universe would be finite in volume. The reason for a finite volume is that a straight line extended indefinitely in what is called *spherical geometry* will eventually return to the place from which it started. That is, a person projected in a straight line by a space vehicle in some direction will eventually return to his starting place from the opposite direction. A straight line "bends" with a certain radius, the radius being a description of the size of the universe. In this kind of universe there would be no edges and there would be no empty space; the whole universe could be filled up with galaxies and stars and, at the same time, would have a finite number of galaxies and stars and a finite volume. Noneuclidean geometry, therefore, provides a possible way of explaining the known features of what, on some grounds, seems to be a finite universe.

These special types of geometry are virtually impossible to visualize because we are so completely used to thinking in terms of euclidean space. But consider a historical analogy. Not many years ago there were still some people who thought the earth was flat. When a scientist would say, "The earth is round; so if you go west far enough, you will end up in the East," these people just could not understand. They pointed out that the earth "looks" flat and it was unnatural to think otherwise, the way one might now argue that the world looks euclidean and it is unnatural to imagine the alternatives. Just as we now know that the earth is round, it has no edges, and its surface area is finite, so did Einstein argue that the universe is spherical, it has no edges, and its volume is finite. The main difference is that, for the earth, we are talking about two-dimensional curvature, whereas, for space, Einstein talked about three-dimensional curvature. Another difference is that, for the earth, we have demonstrated the truth of this idea, whereas no one has yet proved beyond doubt the existence of curvature for the universe.

So, what is the geometry of the universe? We don't know for sure. We aren't even too sure whether this question can be asked because the universe may not be homogeneous and the geometry may be different in different locations. There are many possibilities of com-

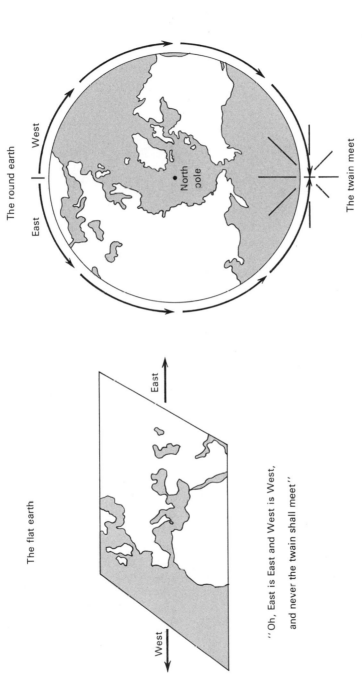

The flat earth

The round earth

East   West

• North pole

West   East

The twain meet

"Oh, East is East and West is West,

and never the twain shall meet"

Figure 8   The flat earth and the round earth, examples of how two-dimensional space curvature acts.

$$90° + 90° + 90° \neq 180°$$

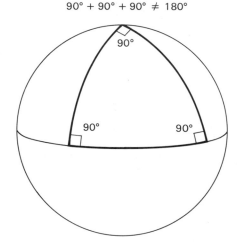

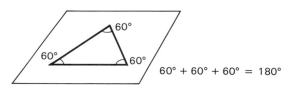

$$60° + 60° + 60° = 180°$$

Figure 9   The sums of the angles in a triangle on a flat surface and on a sphere.

plication in cosmology that astronomers prefer not to think about, for the present. They first want to see what the large-scale overall structure is, as it can best be represented.

In addition to the problem of the boundary of the universe, there is one further question regarding its nature, and that concerns the time problem. When we observe the universe, we are observing light emitted by various parts of the universe at various distances; but, since light doesn't travel instantaneously, when we look at very distant objects we aren't seeing what they look like now. Instead we see what they looked like many years ago, according to their distances. The most-distant galaxies that we can examine are seen as they looked billions of years ago. We have a picture of the universe that isn't really a snapshot; it isn't a picture of what the universe

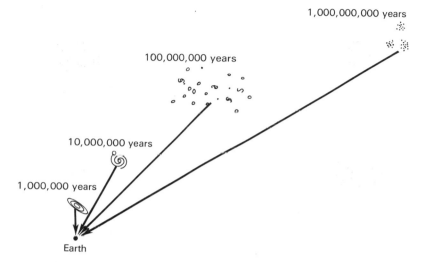

1,000,000,000 years

100,000,000 years

10,000,000 years

1,000,000 years

Earth

Figure 10   *The time problem: the most distant clusters are seen by us as they looked long long ago. (Not to scale.)*

looks like "now," rather it is a historical parade of events and conditions, from the beginning (if there was one) to the present.

Corrections have to be made for the time problem. For instance, when measuring a galaxy at a very large distance, it is necessary to calculate what it looks like now, knowing something about how gal-

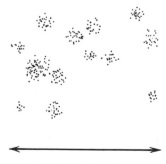

1,000,000,000,000,000,000,000 miles

Figure 11   *An example of the arrangement of clusters of galaxies in a supercluster.*

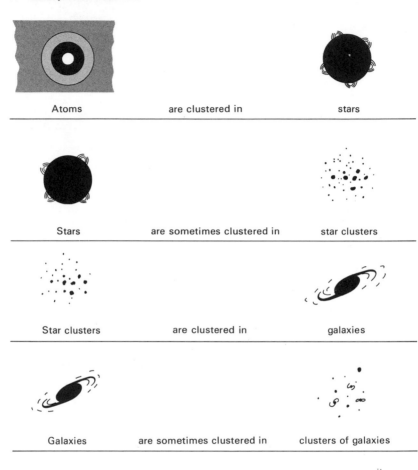

Atoms	are clustered in	stars
Stars	are sometimes clustered in	star clusters
Star clusters	are clustered in	galaxies
Galaxies	are sometimes clustered in	clusters of galaxies
Clusters of galaxies	are sometimes clustered in	clusters of clusters of galaxies

Figure 12 The clustering hierarchy.

Figure 13   A cluster of galaxies in the constellation Pegasus.

Figure 14   A large galaxy (M 31) with two small galaxy companions (M 32 above and NGC 205 below, right). This is the nearest spiral galaxy to ours.

Figure 15 Individual stars, star clouds, and clusters seen in one of the spiral arms of the galaxy shown in Figure 14.

axies evolve. A galaxy, for instance, that sent out its light 4 or 5 billion years ago is now probably a very different sort of thing from what it was when it sent out the light we see. The time problem is a rather serious one, and there isn't any way of getting around it.

The last point about the nature of the universe concerns its contents. In cosmology, mathematicians often prefer to work with a universe that has no contents because it is much easier to do the mathematics with an empty universe. For a more realistic approach these mathematicians will sometimes add a little something to their universe in the form of matter, but they spread it out completely homogeneously. We know that this is almost, but not quite exactly, the case.

How is the matter distributed in the universe? Although we don't yet know the answer in exact detail, we know the basic properties of this distribution. It is clear that, on a very large scale, the universe seems to be made up of clusters of objects, and each of these objects is a cluster of smaller objects, which are clusters of still smaller objects, which are clusters of even smaller ones. Apparently there is a high degree of clustering in the universe. The largest clusters that have been detected so far (besides the universe itself, of course) are the clusters of clusters of galaxies, sometimes called *superclusters*. They are made up of between 5 and 40 clusters of galaxies. The sizes of these superclusters are immense, averaging about 100 million light years, where a light year is the distance light travels in one year at the speed of 186,000 miles per *second*.

The clusters of galaxies are smaller objects, "only" a few million light years across on the average, and the galaxies are comparatively quite small, only about 100,000 light years in diameter. Nevertheless, such a typical galaxy contains about a million million stars, each one, on the average, 100 or so times the size of the earth. So, as we see, the universe is not truly empty.

CHAPTER 2

THE SIZE
OF THE
UNIVERSE

The universe is so vast that it is a very difficult and complicated thing to measure. Figure 16 shows a "scale pyramid," which illustrates the various stages in the derivation of the extremely large distances involved in measuring the observable universe. This pyramid is a structure that depends ultimately on its foundations, which are the measurements made nearest to the earth. Each step in the structure depends on its own foundations; so if there is any weakness anywhere in the structure, if any of the scientific arguments are incorrect or inaccurate, then the very top of the structure is incorrect by the cumulative amount. There is no way that we can just go out and measure the universe independently of many other parts of astronomy.

We find the universe to be extremely large. The most distant cluster of galaxies measured is about 200,000,000,000,000,000,000,000 miles (or about 500 million light years) away from us. Astronomers, who often deal with very large numbers like these, employ a shorthand notation for them to avoid writing out all those zeros. For instance, instead of writing 1,000,000, you can write 10^6, where the 6, called the *exponent* of ten, tells how many zeros follow the "1." Thus, the distance of the cluster of galaxies can be written 2×10^{23} miles, instead of 200,000,000,000,000,000,000,000, miles.

To measure these distances, some sort of distance scale near the

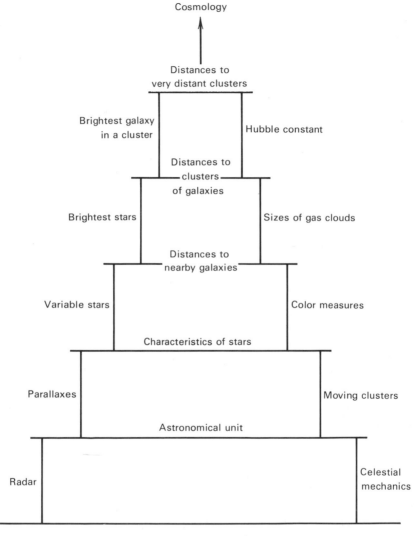

Figure 16   The distance-scale pyramid.

earth must first be established. In the past this was a very difficult task, but recently a new and simple method has been used to establish the local solar system distance scale. A few years ago *radar* methods proved to be so much more accurate than the older classical methods that it is the prime source of such information now.

How can radar be used to establish the distance scale near the earth? One simply sends a radar pulse to some nearby object, for example, the moon, and then waits until that signal is reflected back from the moon and reaches the radar-detecting instrument. Then, since the velocity of the radar pulse is known (it is the velocity of light in outer space) and since the time elapsed between sending and receiving the signals can be measured very accurately, the distance to the moon can be calculated. This was first done in the early

Figure 17   Measuring the distance to the moon by radar.

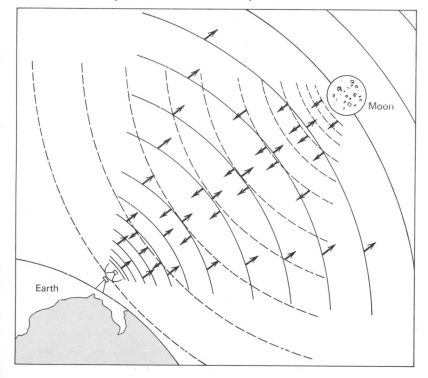

1960s, with the result that the moon at mean distance is now known to be 384,402 kilometers away with an accuracy of ±1.5 kilometers. More recently, radar has been used to measure the distances to the planets Venus and Mars, and, because of improved techniques, the accuracy there is even better; for instance, the distance to Venus is known to an accuracy of 0.0001 percent.

Of course, radar measures the distance to the moon or to a planet only at the particular time we happen to measure it. But it also tells us much more than that if we use "celestial mechanics" (what astronomers call the application of Newton's law of gravity to the motions of astronomical objects). From celestial mechanics we find out that, if we know the distance between the earth and the moon or between the earth and any planet at any particular time, then the

Figure 18   The relationship between the periods and the radii of the orbits of the planets.

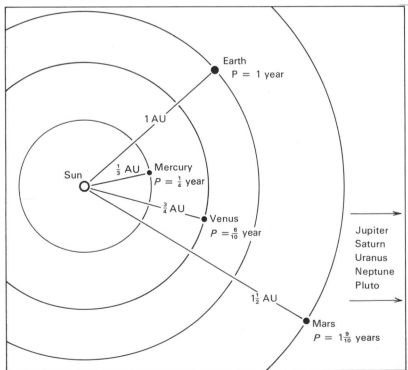

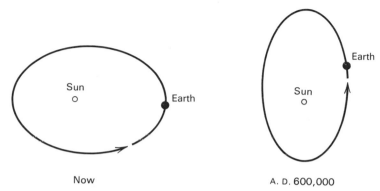

Now   A. D. 600,000

Figure 19   A view of the earth's orbit now and in 600,000 years, after it has been perturbed by the other planets. The eccentricity is exaggerated.

whole distance problem is solved for the solar system. According to Newton's law, this distance is related to the period of the planet around the sun (or of the moon around the earth) in an accurately known way; so we can immediately find the *relative* distances of all planets just from their accurately and easily measured periods. Thus, all we need to know is one distance at one time to get the distance scale for the entire solar system.

Unfortunately if we want to get accuracies as good as 0.0001 percent, several other problems enter in and must be taken into account. In the first place, we have to make the radar-timing measurement that accurately. Second, we have to know the velocity of light with that accuracy. Third, we have to know the nature of the changing orbit of the planet, which we can determine only by repeated measurements for many centuries. The planets all have orbits that change with time because of the influence of the other planets on them. This is a terribly difficult problem, but, fortunately, most of the planets have been observed with high accuracy for more than a century; also, the science of celestial mechanics has developed to the point where, with special high-speed computing machines, we can carry out the difficult mathematics involved. Fourth, we have to know the orbit of the earth as a function of time because it too is changing with time. Fifth, we have to know the radius of the earth accurately because everything has to be corrected to the center of the earth. If we have our observatory, say, in Massachusetts, then the distance measured is wrong because the orbit of the earth is not the orbit of Massachusetts; it is the orbit of the center of the earth. We have to know exactly where Massachusetts is with respect to the center of the earth, which is a measure of the earth's radius. Sixth, we have to know the law of gravitation, which Newton formulated. Fortunately it is very simple. Of course, there are small corrections to it imposed by general relativity, but for the planets Venus and Mars these corrections are not large. For the planet Mercury they become very much more important, and the effects of general relativity have to be taken into account. *All* these things have to be known with a high degree of accuracy before we can solve the problem of the solar system distance scale.

People have done these things, and we have, therefore, a firm foundation for the distance scale of the universe. An extremely important number that comes out of this radar measurement is the mean radius of the earth's orbit, a number so important that it is called the *astronomical unit*. This unit is the basis for the next portion of the distance-scale structure because, as will be shown, we can measure the distances to the nearest stars with it by using trigonometry.

First, let us look at what used to be the method of finding the value of the astronomical unit, since it is similar to what is still being done for stars. The earth has a certain size, and, if we observe a planet from two different observatories at different places on the earth, we can measure its distance by comparing its positions against the background stars, which are very much more distant. This is called *parallax*. Actually, it has been found, even the nearest planets are so far away that we can't accurately measure their distances using the method of parallax. But there are other bodies in the solar system, and among them are small objects called *asteroids,* most only about as big as a house (the *largest* has a diameter of 500 miles). They have orbits that are in between those of the planets, most of them exterior to the earth. A few asteroids come quite close to the earth, however, and one of those that approaches quite near is the asteroid Eros. It comes close enough to the earth that we can measure its distance quite accurately by the parallax method. After determining Eros' orbit by observing it a sufficient length of time, we can then find the list of things one needs to determine the scale, we can get the absolute scale of its orbit and of the earth's, and we can mea-

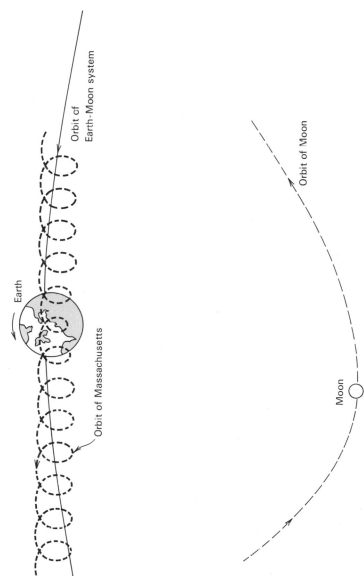

Figure 20 The orbit of Massachusetts around the sun is influenced by the rotation of the earth and by the revolution of the earth and the moon around the center of gravity of the earth-moon system.

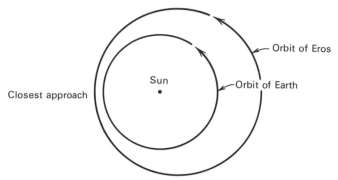

Figure 21   The orbit of the asteroid Eros.

sure the astronomical unit. That was what was done until radar methods became possible.

The *parallax* principle can also be used on a much greater scale. Consider the earth's orbit around the sun. In October, for instance, the earth is on one side of its orbit, and six months later the earth is opposite that position. If, on October 1, we take a photograph of a star and measure its position against the background stars that are very much farther away, and then, on April 1, take a photograph of this star and measure its position again, we will find its position to

Figure 22   How two observatories can measure the distance to Eros by triangulation. (Not to scale.)

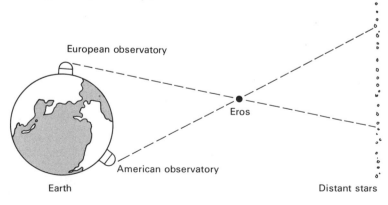

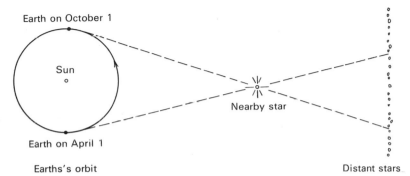

Earth on October 1

Sun
o

Earth on April 1

Nearby star

Earths's orbit

Distant stars

Figure 23 How the distance to a nearby star can be measured from the earth by triangulation.

have changed; by using trigonometry, the amount of change will tell us the distance to the star. We just measure the triangle formed by the two positions of the earth and the star. The amount the star appeared to move is a measure of the angle; so we can construct the triangle and find the distance immediately. There are a sufficiently large number of stars close to the sun that we now know accurately the distances, by the parallax method, of about a thousand stars. We know the distances less accurately of several thousand more which are more distant. The parallax method takes us out to distances of

Figure 24 How we can measure the distance to a nearby galaxy by triangulation, if we are very patient.

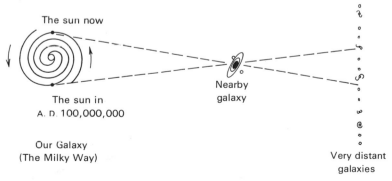

The sun now

The sun in
A. D. 100,000,000

Our Galaxy
(The Milky Way)

Nearby
galaxy

Very distant
galaxies

Convergent
point

Hyades cluster

Figure 25   *The proper motions of stars in the Hyades cluster and the point toward which they seem to converge. Motions shown are for 100,000 years.*

about 500 light years. That is not a very large distance as far as the universe is concerned, but it is quite a distance compared to the scale of the solar system. It gives us distances to stars, though still not to very many.

How accurate is this method? For the nearest star, the accuracy is something on the order of 1 percent. That is much worse, of course, than one in a million, but, still, it is good considering the vast distance involved. However, as we go farther off, the accuracy becomes worse and becomes entirely hopeless by the time we get to 500 light years or so. We can use it with a high degree of accuracy for only a few of the stars in our own local Galaxy.

What do we do after that? Well, unfortunately, we can't use the parallax principle any more, although it is true that the sun revolves around the center of our Galaxy. The sun's period of revolution is

Figure 26   *The method by which the distance to the Hyades can be measured by comparing the apparent motions and the convergent-point position.*

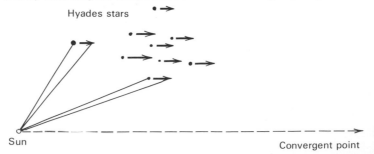

Hyades stars

Sun

Convergent point

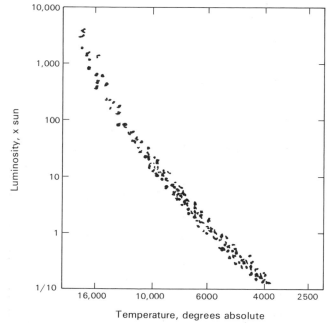

Figure 27   The main sequence of stars.

about 100 million years; so we would have to wait about that long between photographs to take advantage of the principle of parallax for other galaxies. This is too long, of course; so we go to other methods.

Because the other methods are less simple and involve many different types of evidence, many intermediate steps are required before we can find the distance to even the nearest galaxies. The first step takes us just a little beyond the most distant stars for which really accurate parallaxes can be obtained. This is a very important and fundamental step, yet it involves mainly only one small group of stars, gathered together in a single cluster, called the *Hyades*. The Hyades cluster is sufficiently close to the sun (about 130 light years) that we can measure accurately the motions of the individual members and can see how these motions differ from one side of the cluster to the other. The apparent motions of the stars of the Hyades appear to converge toward a point off to one side. This is because

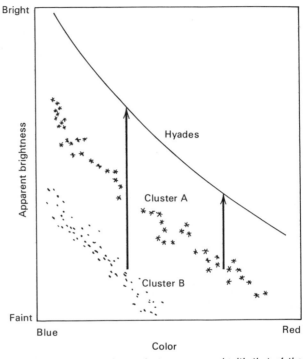

Figure 28   The main sequences of two clusters compared with that of the Hyades. The distance to the two clusters is obtained by measuring how much fainter than the Hyades the main sequence appears.

the entire cluster is moving away from the sun with a moderate velocity, and, since all stars in the cluster are moving approximately in the same direction, their paths are parallel. The distance to the cluster can be determined immediately by combining a knowledge of the direction of the convergent point, which is the direction of motion of the entire cluster, with the line-of-sight motion, which can be measured spectrographically (Chapter 3) by the doppler effect. In this way, a very accurate measurement of the distance to the Hyades cluster is possible simply by measuring the motions of its individual stars.

With a knowledge of the distance to the Hyades cluster and with the realization that all the stars of the cluster are at approximately the same distance, it is possible to determine the intrinsic proper-

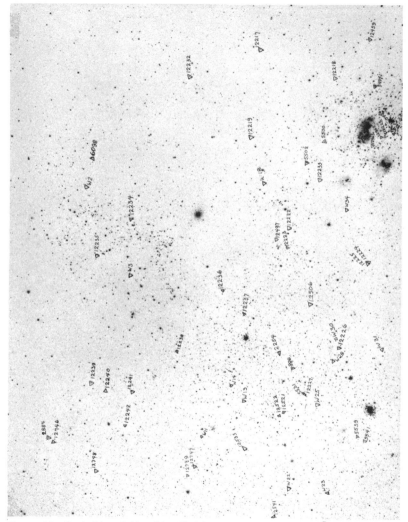

Figure 29   Cepheid variables identified in a portion of a nearby galaxy
(the Large Magellanic Cloud).

ties of a wide variety of stars—in fact, of all the types of stars found in this cluster. It is found that the Hyades stars show a strict relationship between luminosity and temperature. These normal stars make up what is called the *main sequence.* The known distance to the Hyades allows us to measure the true luminosity of any main sequence star in the universe if we can determine its temperature.

Using the Hyades as the basis, it is now possible, knowing the characteristics of various types of stars, to carry the distance-scale calibration one step further. For instance, now we can measure the distances to other star clusters at greater distances than the Hyades for which the motions are not accurately measurable. Going to such more-distant clusters allows us to increase the range of calibration of properties of more and more different kinds of stars. In all cases, the basic reference is to the temperature-luminosity relationship found for the main sequence stars in the Hyades. The nearest stars to the sun for which parallaxes can be measured also aid in this calibration procedure of the main sequence.

After many kinds of stars, represented by a study of many different types of star clusters, have been calibrated in this way, it is pos-

Figure 30   The light curve of a Cepheid variable star in the Large Magellanic Cloud. The period of the star is about four days.

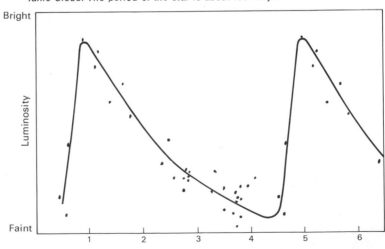

Time, days

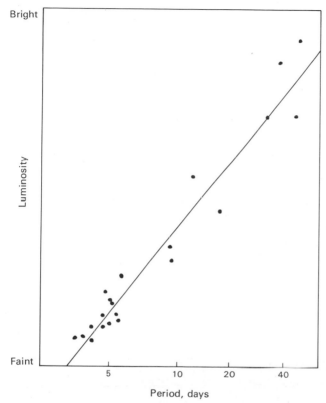

Figure 31   *The relationship between period and luminosity for Cepheids in the Large Magellanic Cloud.*

sible to take a much larger step and measure the distances to the nearest galaxies. It is found that certain types of stars vary in brightness in a regular way. These are called *Cepheid variables* and *RR Lyrae variables,* and several of them exist in clusters that are calibrated by the Hyades. They can also be found in the nearest gal-axies, and, since these stars have periods of variability that are re-lated to their true intrinsic luminosity, they are excellent distance indicators. Thus the next step is a large one, but a reliable one, and the variable stars give us good estimates of distances to a fairly large number of nearby galaxies—roughly 20 all told.

From a survey of all the nearby galaxies for which distances can be estimated as above, it is found that the most luminous and conspicuous objects in these galaxies can also be used as distance indicators in one further step. In particular, the luminosities of the very brightest stars in the galaxy turn out to be fairly uniform from galaxy to galaxy and can be used as distance indicators up to even larger distances. Similarly, the sizes of the immense clouds of hot glowing gas that are found in galaxies also tend to be similar from one galaxy to the next; so, simply by measuring the diameters of the largest of such gas clouds in more distant galaxies, it is possible to determine the distance to them. Using either the method of brightest stars or the sizes of gas clouds in the galaxy, it is possible to go out to vast distances, as far away as about 30 million light years.

Beyond that distance, two independent methods of getting distances become possible. First, it is found that galaxies are moving away from us with greater and greater velocities the greater the distances. This is found to be the case for galaxies as far away as we can detect them; so one estimate of the distance to a galaxy comes immediately from a measurement of its velocity (Chapter 3). An independent measure of the distance to very distant galaxies can

Figure 32 A Cepheid variable in the Large Magellanic Cloud, shown at maximum (left) and at minimum (right).

Figure 33   A nearby galaxy (M 33), the brightest stars of which can be seen and can be used to measure its distance.

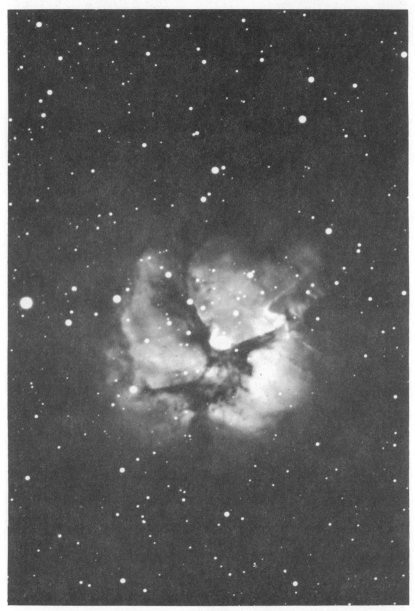

Figure 34   A large gas cloud (NGC 6514) in our Galaxy.

Figure 35 Large gas clouds in a distant galaxy (NGC 2403).

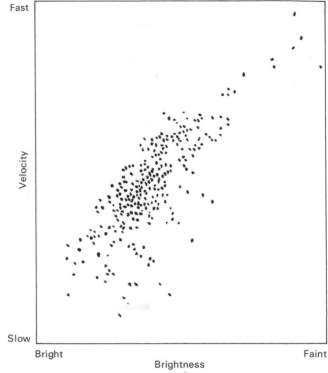

Fast

Velocity

Slow

Bright   Faint

Brightness

Figure 36   The relationship between radial velocity and distance for galaxies.

Figure 37   A distant cluster of galaxies. The arrow points to the brightest member, which can be used to measure the distance to the cluster.

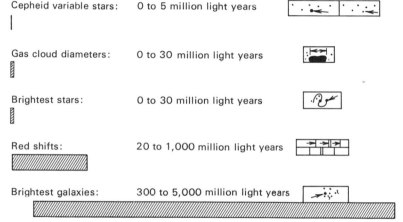

Figure 38   *The ranges for different methods of distance determinations of galaxies.*

come when the galaxies are members of a cluster. Just as the brightest star in a galaxy can be used as a criterion of luminosity, it is likewise true that the brightest galaxy in a cluster of galaxies can be used as a criterion of distance. In neither case is the accuracy very great, sometimes having an uncertainty factor as large as 2 or 3. Nevertheless, the combination of velocity measurement and brightest-galaxies-in-a-cluster measurement leads us to very very distant galaxies, at the limit of our observing capabilities. Furthermore, it is the comparison between these two measurements that will eventually lead us to the solution of the problem of cosmology and the answer to the question: What is the size and shape of the universe?

CHAPTER 3

THE EXPANSION OF THE UNIVERSE

For many years it was thought that the universe was pretty much static. Aside from the motions of planets and stars in their orbits, no motions on a large scale were expected, certainly not for the universe as a whole. Yet, in about 1920, when the first velocities of galaxies were measured, it was found that the observable universe is moving, and this motion is in the form of outward expansion.

The expansion of the universe can be detected through a physical effect called the *doppler shift,* which arises whenever a source of light has velocity with respect to the observer. Most people are very familiar with the doppler effect as it applies to sounds emitted by trains and airplanes. A train whistle, for instance, is higher when the train is approaching and lower as it is receding. The reason is simply that the wavelength of the sound heard is affected by the velocity of the object emitting this wavelength; so the approaching train seems to have a whistle with a shorter wavelength, and a departing train seems to have a whistle with a longer wavelength. Similarly for light, the wavelength that is measured is also dependent upon the velocity of the object. There is a formula that relates this dependence and allows us to calculate the velocity of any object for which we can measure a known wavelength.

Now, in the case of a train, if we are curious to know what the velocity of the train is, all we need do is stop it, blow the whistle, measure the wavelength of the sound, and then start the train going again at the velocity we want to measure. Then we measure the apparent wavelength of the whistle and, if it is leaving us, it will be longer (lower in tone). How much longer it is depends upon the velocity; so if it is extremely fast it will be extremely long. We can calculate the change by using what is called the *doppler formula*. The approximate form of this equation states that the velocity of the source can be found by multiplying the velocity of the wave (sound or light) by the change in wavelength and dividing this by the original, or true, wavelength. If, for a train whistle, for instance, with a particular wavelength, for example, middle C (wavelength 4.2 feet) we find that it sounds like D above middle C (wavelength 3.7 feet), then the velocity of the train is found to be simply the velocity of sound (1,100 feet per second) times 4.2 minus 3.7, all divided by 4.2. This gives a velocity for the train of 131 feet per second, or 89 miles per hour.

To give another example of an application of the doppler effect, let us examine a hypothetical legal brief concerning a case that was brought up in traffic court. A man was arrested for going through a red light. When he was brought before the judge he pleaded, knowing a little physics, that, as a matter of fact, as he was approaching this light it looked green to him because of the doppler effect: green light has a shorter wavelength than red light. Now the judge also knew about the doppler effect; furthermore, he knew the formula,

Figure 39 The expanding universe. Only the distance between the galaxies grows.

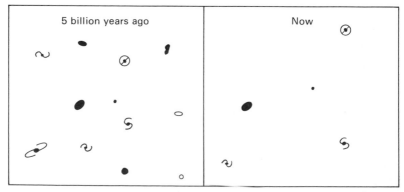

Stationary train

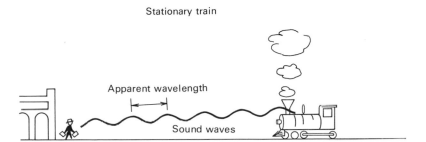

Approaching train

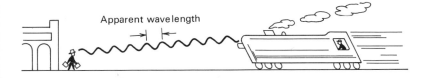

Departing train

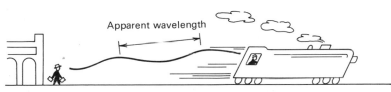

Figure 40   The doppler effect. The whistle of the approaching train sounds higher than that of the departing train.

which apparently the motorist had forgotten. In that particular city, one is fined 10 dollars for every mile per hour that he travels over the speed limit; so the judge quickly set the fine at 1 billion dollars. His reason was simply this: the wavelength of red light is about 6,000 angstroms, and the wavelength of green light is about 5,000 angstroms; so the change in wavelength is 1,000 angstroms. (An angstrom is 10^{-10} meters, or about 6×10^{-14} miles.) The original wave-

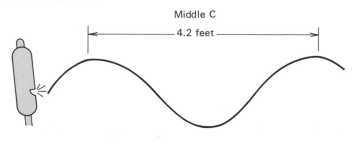

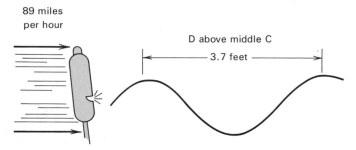

Figure 41   *Middle C blown on a train traveling at 89 miles per hour sounds like D above middle C.*

length was 6,000 angstroms, and the velocity of light is 186,000 miles per second; when this is multiplied out and changed to miles per hour it gives a speed for the car of about 100,000,000 (10^8) miles per hour, finable at 10 dollars each mile per hour.

In astronomy, the doppler effect is extremely useful. We can measure the velocities of stars and galaxies by means of the wavelength shift of their light. None of these objects, galaxies or stars, emits only one wavelength, like a train, but, instead, emits an entire spectrum of light, interrupted here and there by dark (absorption) lines and bright (emission) lines. A particular dark line might be caused by the absorption of that wavelength of light by atoms of calcium, another one by hydrogen, and so on. We identify these lines by their arrangement in the spectrum, and then we measure their rest wavelength in the laboratory with a spectrograph, a device that separates light into a complete spectrum of wavelengths. Knowing its rest wavelength, we take the difference, use the doppler formula, and

Figure 42 An emission-line spectrum produced by a hot glowing gas.

find out the velocity of the celestial source. For stars in our Galaxy the velocities are usually small (in astronomical terms), only a few miles per second, usually only 20 or less.

However, for galaxies the situation becomes much more interesting. We find that galaxies are moving with respect to one another with very high velocities. Even in just the local neighborhood of our Galaxy, there are large "peculiar" motions. Here "peculiar" is used in a scientific sense that is a little different from its common meaning. By peculiar motions we mean the actual individual motions after *systematic* motions have been subtracted out. We find that the peculiar motions of galaxies are on the order of 200 to 300 miles per second (about 1,000,000 miles per hour).

Of course, all we can measure with the doppler effect is that component of motion in the "line of sight," that is, in the direction in which we are looking. In the cases of stars we can do more, especially for stars near the sun. In addition to the doppler shift, we can measure the velocity across the sky (perpendicular to the line of sight) by taking a photograph now, and then another one several years later and measuring the displacement. However, galaxies are so much farther away that to measure any such displacement for

Figure 43 An absorption-line spectrum produced by a cooler gas in front of a hot source (the atmosphere of the sun in front of the sun).

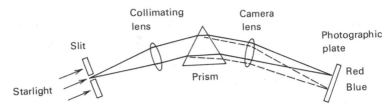

Figure 44 How a spectrograph, using a prism, separates light of different wavelengths.

them would take millions of years. Therefore, all we know for galaxies is the velocity in the line-of-sight direction.

When we look farther and farther away, at doppler shifts of more and more distant galaxies, we find that the spectrum lines move systematically farther and farther to the red. This is called the *red shift* of the galaxies. Since red is a long wavelength, this trend means that the distant galaxies are moving away from us. At distances beyond about 35 million light years, all galaxies are moving away from us, and beyond this the velocities get greater and greater. At smaller distances the peculiar motions of the galaxies are larger than the systematic outward velocities; so the red shift is difficult to detect. Although accurate measurement of distances to galaxies is difficult beyond about 35 million light years, we can use some of the less-accurate distance indicators to continue out farther. We find that the relationship is extremely good, and what we have, in effect, is a law of nature, a close correlation between velocity and distance for galaxies.

For nearby objects, where we can use the brightest stars and the variable stars for distances, we find that individual galaxies have velocities of only a few hundred miles per second. As we go out to more distant clusters, where we use the brightest galaxy in a cluster as a distance criterion, we find larger and larger velocities, up to 100,000 miles per second. At the limit of our measurement capabilities we find the velocity becoming very large, almost as large as the velocity of light. The velocity-distance relationship, called *Hubble's law*, is described by a very simple formula: the velocity is equal to the distance multiplied by a constant (abbreviated by an *H*). This constant, called the *Hubble constant,* was derived for the first time

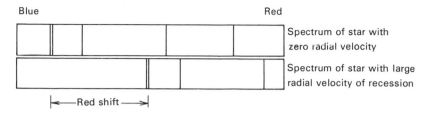

Figure 45 How the radial velocity of a star is measured.

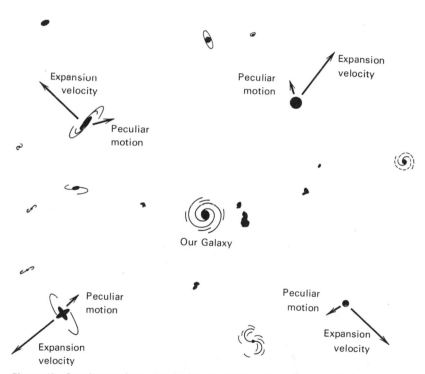

Figure 46 Peculiar motions of galaxies are small and random in orientation.

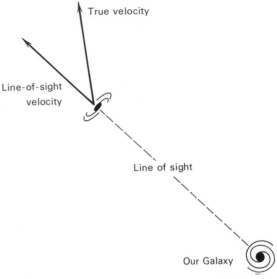

Figure 47   The line-of-sight (radial) velocity is not necessarily the true velocity.

by Edwin Hubble, an astronomer at the Mt. Wilson Observatory in California.

As an example, consider the nearby large cluster of galaxies in the constellation of Virgo. We measure its distance by the methods of Chapter 2 and find that it has a distance of 35 million light years, a value based mostly on the luminosity of the brightest stars in the individual galaxies in the cluster. The spectra of the Virgo cluster galaxies show a red shift from which we calculate a velocity away from us of 700 miles per second, on the average. Now, using the Virgo cluster, we can calibrate Hubble's law by determining rather accurately the value of H. As you can see, it turns out to be about 20 miles per second per million light years.

Now we can apply Hubble's law to any other galaxy. Let's take, for instance, a cluster of galaxies so far away that even the 200-inch Palomar telescope, the largest in the world, has difficulty in obtaining spectra of the members. If we have no other measure of the cluster's distance, we can use Hubble's law to get one by measuring its doppler shift. We will have to sit in the cage (the observer's capsule at the upper end of the telescope) of the 200-inch telescope all night long during a long winter night to expose our photographic plate in our spectrograph to get a usable spectrum of the brightest galaxy in this very faint cluster of galaxies. After we develop our photograph, we will find a tiny spectrum on it that we can look at with a microscope. We will see on this spectrum the lines shifted so far to the red that the velocity must be about 40,000 miles per second. We then know immediately that the distance to this cluster is 2 billion (2×10^9) light years.

Because the doppler formula given above is really only the approximation of a more complicated formula, it turns out that, if we go to much faster velocities than this, we no longer can use it. Also, the geometry of the universe enters into the calculations; so the formulas become very much more complicated and even, to a certain extent, unknown.

Aside from this problem, how far away can we measure velocities

Figure 48   The spectrum of a galaxy is often extremely small and hard to distinguish.

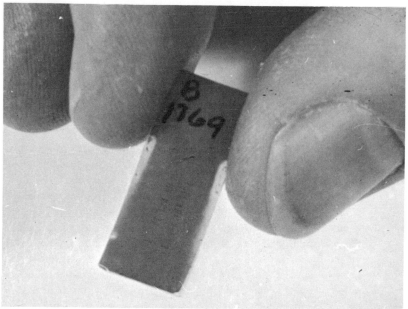

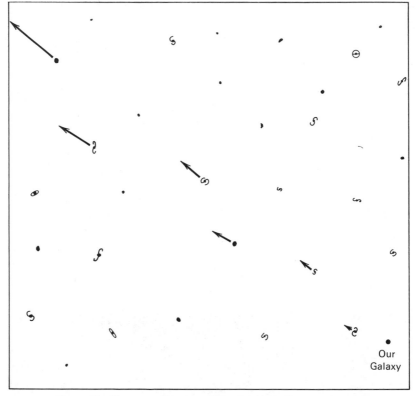

Figure 49   The more distant a galaxy, the faster its recession.

to explore the general expansion of the universe? How distant are the farthest galaxies for which a red shift can be measured? A cluster at a distance of about 2 billion light years is just about the most distant cluster for which it has been possible to obtain spectra of *normal* galaxies. The reason we cannot take spectra of more-distant ones is simply that the night sky, even at the best observatory sites, has a certain luminosity of its own. It looks dark but it is not completely black, and when we use a very powerful telescope with a powerful spectrograph and are trying to photograph something extremely faint, the night sky appears brighter than this faint object and gives a spectrum of itself instead. This essentially overexposes

Figure 50   Two spiral galaxies in the Virgo cluster.

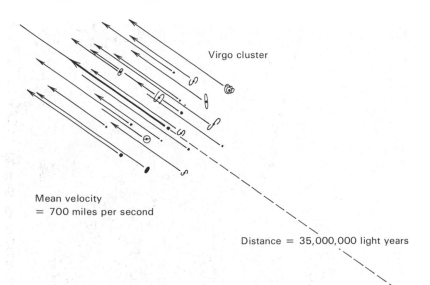

Virgo cluster

Mean velocity
= 700 miles per second

Distance = 35,000,000 light years

Our Galaxy

Figure 51   The mean velocity of the galaxies in the Virgo cluster is a calibration of the Hubble constant.

Figure 52   Distances of clusters of galaxies.

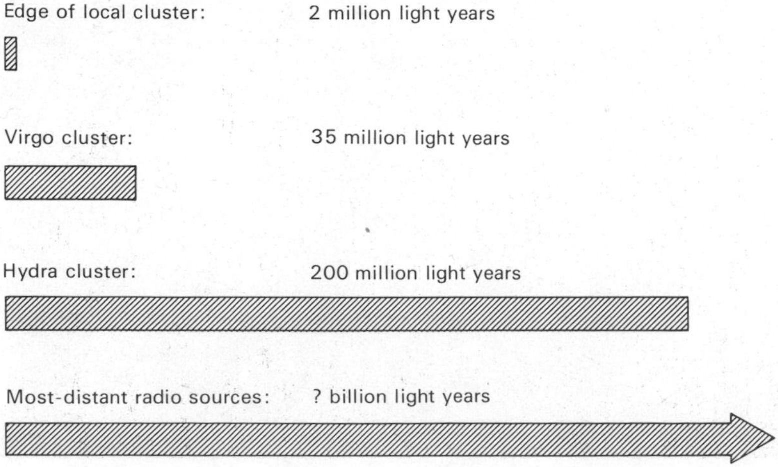

Edge of local cluster: 2 million light years

Virgo cluster: 35 million light years

Hydra cluster: 200 million light years

Most-distant radio sources: ? billion light years

the plate; so we cannot see the spectrum of the galaxy at all. It would actually be possible to expose the plate all week, with patience, and just close the shutter in the morning and open it up again at night. By doing this, we should be able to measure spectra of extremely distant galaxies, if it were not for the night sky. But for the largest telescopes the night sky fogs the plate after about 5 to 10 hours, before we have reached much beyond 2 billion light years.

The obvious solution is to get above the night sky—that is, above the upper atmosphere where the night-sky light originates. The way to do this, of course, is to put a telescope out in space. For this work a very large telescope is needed, something on the order of the size of the 200-inch Palomar telescope. Smaller telescopes have already been orbited, and plans to orbit a telescope of this size indicate that it may be done by about 1980. Another place to put it, rather than in the earth's orbit, is on the moon, where there is no atmosphere and where the sky is thus extremely dark. Perhaps an instrument similar to the 200-inch Palomar telescope will be placed on the moon by about 1990. There are all kinds of problems involved in putting telescopes on the moon that we will have to meet when they arise. For example, there will be no atmosphere to protect the telescope (and the astronomer, if any) from being bombarded by cosmic rays and meteorites.

Until then, we have to use another method: the observation of gal-

Figure 53 A highly red-shifted spectrum of a distant galaxy. The galaxy spectrum is the faint line between the two rows of emission lines (placed on the spectrum for comparison).

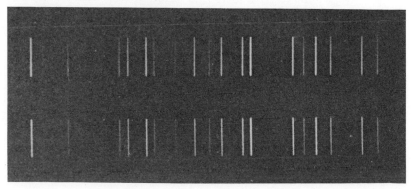

axies that are not normal. A very small percentage of galaxies are experiencing very unusual, but violent, events that we will call *explosions*. We do not yet understand entirely what causes these explosions. There are a dozen theories worked out by imaginative scientists, but none of them fit all the facts, so far. The important thing here is that these explosions result in extremely hot gas clouds in the galaxies, which cause very bright emission lines in their spectra. Emission lines are very easy to measure, much more

Figure 54 The faint smudges at the center of this photograph are the brightest members of a very-distant cluster of galaxies.

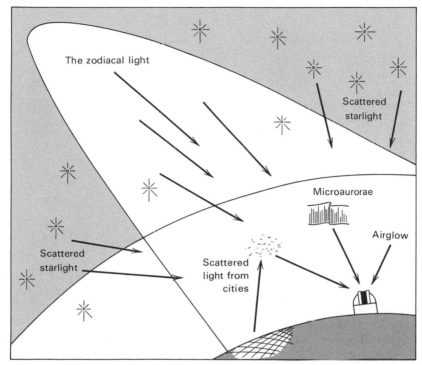

Figure 55   The night sky appears dark but is actually illuminated by many sources.

so than absorption lines; thus, by looking at these peculiar emission-line galaxies, we can go to at least twice the distance otherwise possible. The most-distant emission-line galaxy we have measured has a velocity of 80,000 miles per second, and this places it at a distance of about 4 billion light years.

Though a tremendous distance, this is still not as far as we would like to go because this is not yet far enough to tell us the geometry of the universe. This is only about one-half the velocity of light, and we need to go to eight-tenths or nine-tenths the velocity of light to solve the problem of cosmology. Does this mean that we have to wait many years to go outside the atmosphere with a 200-inch telescope and look at some more-distant emission-line galaxies? Possibly not,

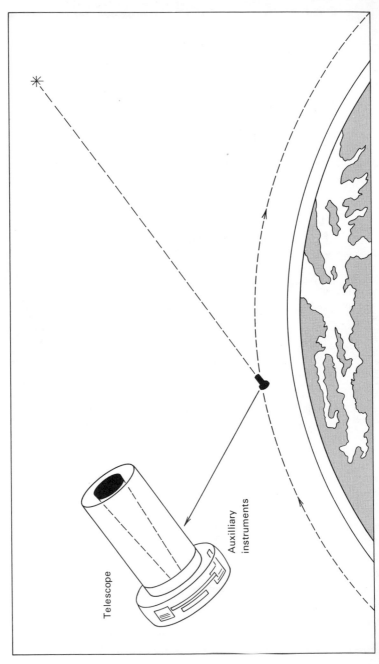

Figure 56   A large orbiting telescope is planned for use in about 1980.

because we have discovered, besides the explosive galaxies, some even more unusual objects. These are the *quasi-stellar objects* (or "quasars" for short), called that because they are so small they almost look like stars. They seem to be up to 100 times more luminous than the most luminous normal galaxies, and they have extremely brilliant emission lines. We do not understand the quasi-stellar objects at all. They are very small, they are very bright, and they are apparently experiencing some superviolent explosion. Some of them are sources of intense radio noise as well.

Although most astronomers believe that quasars obey the Hubble

Figure 57 An observatory on the moon would have to take precautions against damage by meteorites or by cosmic rays.

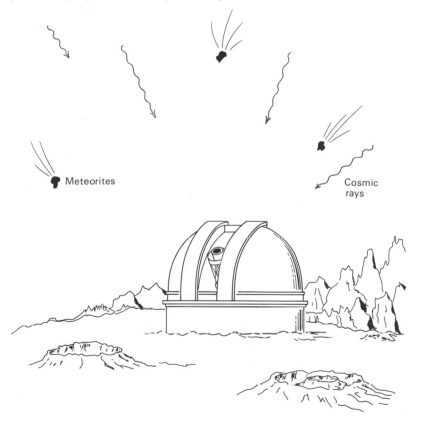

relationship between velocity and distance, it is also possible that they are, instead, much closer objects having high red shifts, either because of a nearby, recent explosion of great violence or because of relativistic effects. At present the evidence, though still confusing and contradictory, favors the idea that the quasars are very distant objects, some of which are receding with enormous velocities.

To date the largest velocity we have measured anywhere is for one of these quasars: 150,000 miles per second, which is eight-tenths the velocity of light. For this system the red shift in the spectrum is

Figure 58   A radio galaxy.

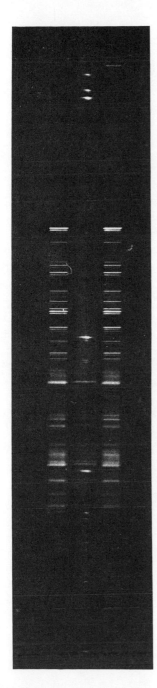

Figure 59   An emission-line spectrum of a peculiar galaxy (NGC 5253).

Figure 60   3C 48, the first-identified very-distant quasar.

twice as big as the wavelength itself. This becomes a rather difficult object to work on for the simple reason that we are looking at a part of the spectrum we have never seen before because it is normally down in the invisible ultraviolet. We sometimes have a difficult time identifying which line is which, especially when we see only a few emission lines.

These quasi-stellar objects are possibly the most-distant things we can see, and we still find that among the faintest ones are those moving away the fastest. This is important because it indicates that the entire universe we can measure and see is in a state of expansion.

What is it expanding from, where is the center, and what caused the expansion? These are questions that cannot yet be answered. We do not know where the center is, and there may not be any. Even

Figure 61   The radio appearance of 3C 273, the nearest quasar, which has an optical and radio jetlike appendage.

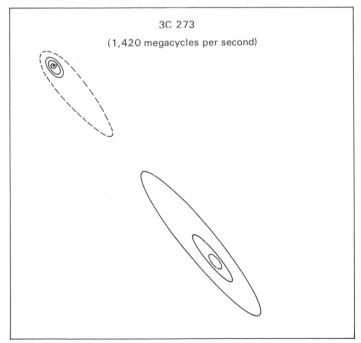

if there is one we may not be able to find it because, when there is a one-to-one correlation between velocity and distance, one cannot detect a center. Think of the simple example of three galaxies: ours, one north of us at, say, 1 million light years, and one south of us at 1 million light years. If they were all together at one time near our Galaxy and are now moving away from us as the center point, we would see what we do: both would have the same distance and the same velocity. But we would also see this if either the north one or the south one had been at the center because then our Galaxy would be moving away with the appropriate velocity and the other noncen-

Figure 62   When galaxies are receding from each other with an apparent velocity proportional to distance, it is impossible to determine which is at the center.

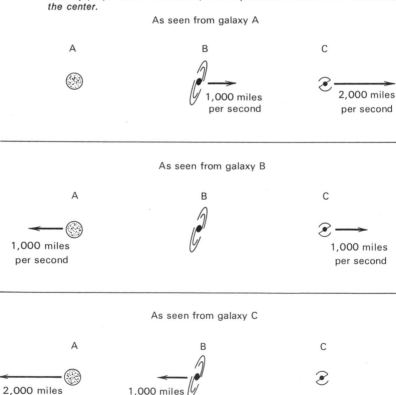

As seen from galaxy A

A   B   C

1,000 miles per second

2,000 miles per second

As seen from galaxy B

A   B   C

1,000 miles per second

1,000 miles per second

As seen from galaxy C

A   B   C

2,000 miles per second

1,000 miles per second

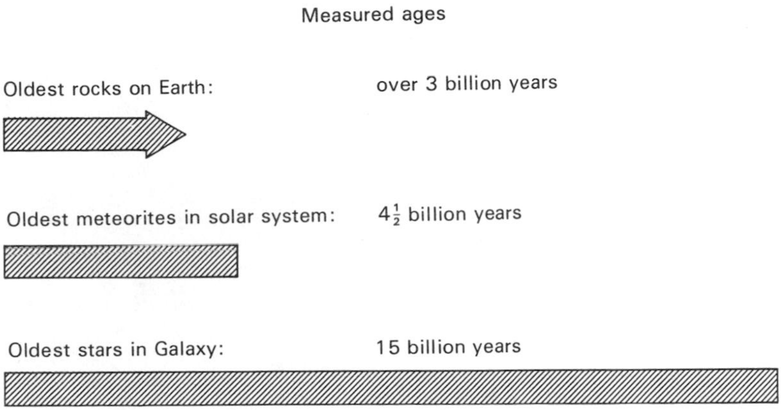

Measured ages

Oldest rocks on Earth: over 3 billion years

Oldest meteorites in solar system: $4\frac{1}{2}$ billion years

Oldest stars in Galaxy: 15 billion years

Figure 63   A comparison of the ages of the earth, the solar system, and our Galaxy.

tral one would be moving with twice that velocity. You simply cannot determine where the center is when there is a correlation like the Hubble law.

We cannot even be sure there is or was a center. If the universe is closed, if it is curved space with a positive curvature making the universe finite in volume, then there is no center, or else every place is its center. Perhaps it is clearest to say that the term "center" doesn't have any definition. After all, the *surface* of the earth doesn't have a center.

What caused the expansion is also something we cannot answer now. In fact, we may never know what went on at the time of the beginning of the expansion because all the clues may have been erased by the violence of the event itself. What happened before that may also be entirely unknowable. Perhaps nothing existed, not even space and time.

It should be mentioned that there are people who believe that something other than expansion is going on. It has been suggested that maybe the red shift we observe is not really due to the doppler effect but is due to something else, some effect we do not know about. This is not really a scientific *theory* because none of the people who have suggested it have come up with a scientifically reasonable idea of just what is causing the red shift. It is just a sugges-

Figure 64   The globular star clusters contain the oldest stars in our Galaxy (NGC 6254).

tion, and, though it cannot yet be treated scientifically, it still may turn out to be correct. Perhaps some day physicists will discover an effect (possibly some kind of fatigue) that occurs over extremely large distances and causes the wavelength of light to shift toward the red, but at the moment we have no such knowledge.

What do we know about the age of the universe? Certainly we can calculate the age of the universe from the expansion rate, and we might suspect that this would be a simple matter. We could just look at the expansion, extrapolate back to the time when all the galaxies were together at one point, and call that the beginning of the universe. The time from that date to now is simply the age of the universe. However, it is, in fact, not quite that simple. We first have to know the geometry of the universe, and then we have to use the very complicated formulas which describe the universe. Each cosmological model gives its own answer; so we will not know the age of the universe until we discover which cosmological theory is correct.

The simplest model of all is the euclidean model of the universe. It has what we think of as normal flat space. It makes everything as simple as possible. Under those circumstances the age is simply 2 divided by 3 times the Hubble constant, which gives us about 7 billion years. This value is not too far from what we know to be the age of the earth. Geologists have shown that the very oldest rocks on the earth are about 4 billion years old. Also, we know from age measurements of meteorites coming to the earth from outer space that the solar system itself has an age of about 4½ billion years; so it is not unreasonable to say the universe as a whole is a little older than that. We would like to think of the solar system as having been in existence a good portion of the time that the universe has been, and it turns out that this would be true if we took these numbers at face value.

One serious difficulty arises, though, if we accept an age of only 7 billion years for the universe. By special, very complicated applications of physics to our knowledge of the evolution of stars, we can measure the ages of stars. When we apply these methods to the stars in our Galaxy, we find that the oldest stars here are 15 billion years old! Of course, there must be something wrong if our Galaxy claims to be older than the universe. There must be some explanation, some error or misinterpretation. Several possibilities exist. One way of avoiding this discrepancy might be to say that the universe is not

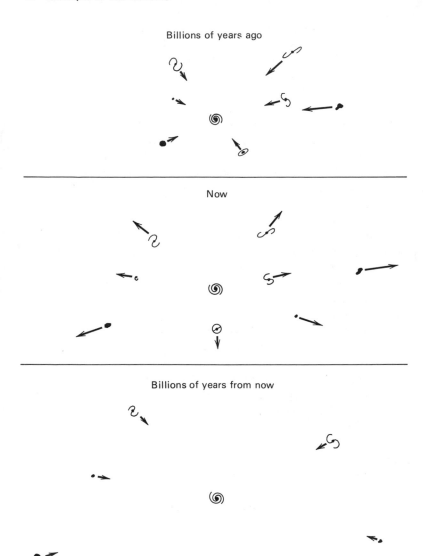

Figure 65   An oscillating universe seen at three times in its history.

euclidean. But if we choose some other geometry and then recalculate the age, it still doesn't completely solve the problem. By stretching things we can get about 10 billion years, but it is very difficult to get it up to 15. Another thing we can say is that the astrophysicists have made some error and the ages of the oldest stars really are not that big. A third alternative is to say that the universe did not originate from a point but is, in fact, oscillating. We just happen to live at a time when it is expanding, but it also contracts. If we can work out a model that contracts to a volume not very much smaller than its present size, when it turns around and expands again, then we can have this going on without affecting the stars in the universe, and we can have stars that are much older than the measured contraction or expansion age. A fourth method of getting around this difficulty is to assume that the universe is infinite in its history and that galaxies are continuously formed to fill up the space left by those moving away. This is the so-called steady-state universe and is one of the various cosmological models that will be described in the next chapter.

CHAPTER
4

MODELS
OF THE
UNIVERSE

Cosmology—the study of the nature of the universe as a whole—involves the construction of hypothetical models of the universe and the testing of these models by comparison with observations. Because of the tremendously complicated nature of the universe, mathematics is the only language capable of describing it adequately. For that reason, most cosmologists are, first and foremost, mathematicians or mathematical physicists, and the approach that they take, of course, is a highly theoretical one. Furthermore, instead of trying to take into account all the known facts, and every little detail, they simplify everything to the point where it can be handled reasonably well mathematically. Among these simplifications are a number of standard assumptions.

First, there is the assumption that the universe is homogeneous —it is a "homogenized universe." This means that matter in the universe is spread out completely uniformly and there are no large-scale clumps or empty spaces. We know, of course, that this is not strictly true. There are large-scale clumps, such as galaxies and clusters of galaxies; but the cosmologists usually take the point of view that they need not worry about these. If they consider a big enough volume, then it is very nearly homogeneous.

The second assumption is that the universe is isotropic. This means that the galaxies are distributed and are moving, whatever

mensionalen Kontinuums können wir uns der Koordinaten ξ_1, ξ_2, ξ_3 bedienen (Projektion auf die Hyperebene $\xi_4 = 0$), da sich vermöge (10) ξ_4 durch ξ_1, ξ_2, ξ_3 ausdrücken läßt. Eliminiert man ξ_4 aus (9), so erhält man für das Linienelement des sphärischen Raumes den Ausdruck

$$
\left.
\begin{aligned}
d\sigma^2 &= \gamma_{\mu\nu}\, d\xi_\mu\, d\xi_\nu \\
\gamma_{\mu\nu} &= \delta_{\mu\nu} + \frac{\xi_\mu \xi_\nu}{R^2 - \rho^2}
\end{aligned}
\right\},
\qquad (11)
$$

wobei $\delta_{\mu\nu} = 1$, wenn $\mu = \nu$, $\delta_{\mu\nu} = 0$, wenn $\mu \neq \nu$, und $\rho^2 = \xi_1^2 + \xi_2^2 + \xi_3^2$ gesetzt wird. Die gewählten Koordinaten sind bequem, wenn es sich um die Untersuchung der Umgebung eines der beiden Punkte $\xi_1 = \xi_2 = \xi_3 = 0$ handelt.

Nun ist uns auch das Linienelement der gesuchten raum-zeitlichen vierdimensionalen Welt gegeben. Wir haben offenbar für die Potentiale $g_{\mu\nu}$, deren beide Indizes von 4 abweichen, zu setzen

$$
g_{\mu\nu} = -\left(\delta_{\mu\nu} + \frac{x_\mu x_\nu}{R^2 - (x_1^2 + x_2^2 + x_3^2)} \right),
\qquad (12)
$$

welche Gleichung in Verbindung mit (7) und (8) das Verhalten von Maßstäben, Uhren und Lichtstrahlen in der betrachteten vierdimensionalen Welt vollständig bestimmt.

§ 4. Über ein an den Feldgleichungen der Gravitation anzubringendes Zusatzglied.

Die von mir vorgeschlagenen Feldgleichungen der Gravitation lauten für ein beliebig gewähltes Koordinatensystem

$$
\left.
\begin{aligned}
G_{\mu\nu} &= -\varkappa \left(T_{\mu\nu} - \frac{1}{2} g_{\mu\nu} T \right) \\
G_{\mu\nu} &= -\frac{\partial}{\partial x_\alpha} \begin{Bmatrix} \mu\nu \\ \alpha \end{Bmatrix} + \begin{Bmatrix} \mu\alpha \\ \beta \end{Bmatrix} \begin{Bmatrix} \nu\beta \\ \alpha \end{Bmatrix} \\
&\quad + \frac{\partial^2 \lg \sqrt{-g}}{\partial x_\mu \partial x_\nu} - \begin{Bmatrix} \mu\nu \\ \alpha \end{Bmatrix} \frac{\partial \lg \sqrt{-g}}{\partial x_\alpha}
\end{aligned}
\right\}
\qquad (13)
$$

Das Gleichungssystem (13) ist keineswegs erfüllt, wenn man für die $g_{\mu\nu}$ die in (7), (8) und (12) gegebenen Werte und für den (kontravarianten) Tensor der Energie der Materie die in (6) angegebenen Werte einsetzt. Wie diese Rechnung bequem auszuführen ist, wird im nächsten Paragraphen gezeigt werden. Wenn es also sicher wäre. daß die von mir bisher benutzten Feldgleichungen (13) die einzigen mit dem Postulat der allgemeinen Relativität vereinbaren wären, so

Figure 66 A page from Einstein's paper (1917) describing his general relativistic cosmological model.

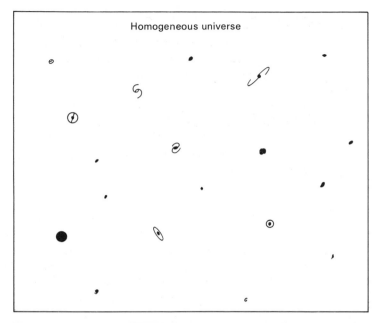

Homogeneous universe

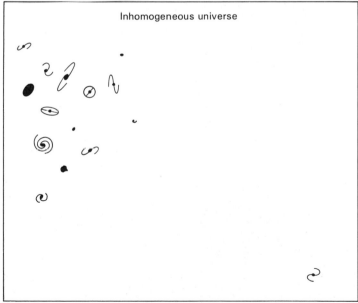

Inhomogeneous universe

Figure 67   Homogeneity.

their velocities, in a smooth and uniform manner. All the velocities, for instance, are velocities of expansion. We don't have a situation where the universe around us is expanding, somewhere else it is contracting, and at other places it is perhaps vibrating or rotating or something else.

The third assumption is that the universe is incoherent. This means that the right hand of the universe doesn't know what the left hand is doing (speaking figuratively, of course, since there is no left or right in the universe). It is not bound together by pressure like a solid or a gas. The effect of any local change or perturbation is only locally felt.

The fourth assumption is uniformity. It is assumed that the universe is uniform in its properties; at extremely large distances the galaxies are different in no fundamental way from those we are measuring in our neighborhood. Only predictable differences, such as the evolution of galaxies (which we can take into account), exist.

The fifth assumption is universality. This means that the laws of physics discovered here on the earth apply throughout the universe. Some cosmologists even go so far as to assume that the laws of physics not only apply throughout the universe but also apply to the universe as a unit, an even bigger assumption.

There have been many different cosmological models put forward in recent years by mathematicians and mathematically oriented astronomers and physicists, and they all involve something about geometry. It was shown in Chapter 1 that there are many kinds of geometry possible and that the particular geometry our universe possesses is not necessarily the geometry of Euclid. In fact, it is a very difficult thing to discover what the geometry of our universe is, and it is the nature of this geometry that is one of the biggest problems in establishing a cosmological model. Different cosmological models take various attitudes toward the problem of geometry. Some leave the question open and some assume a certain geometry, requiring it to be correct if the cosmological model is correct.

The following paragraphs describe several modern models of the universe. Some of these are based on Newton's laws of nature, some are based on Einstein's general relativity, and others are based on still different laws of nature. At the present time it is not yet possible to choose from among these various models. However, it should be emphasized here that each of these cosmological models has been

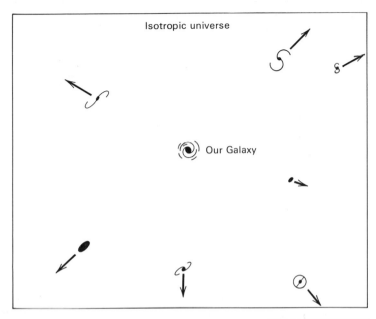

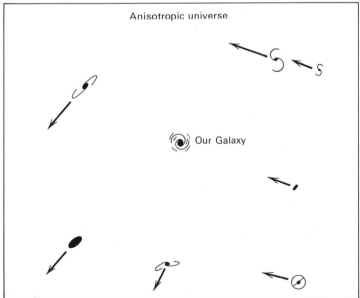

Figure 68   Isotropy.

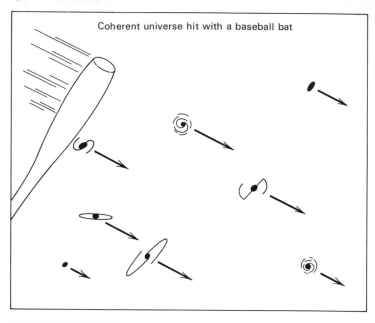

Coherent universe hit with a baseball bat

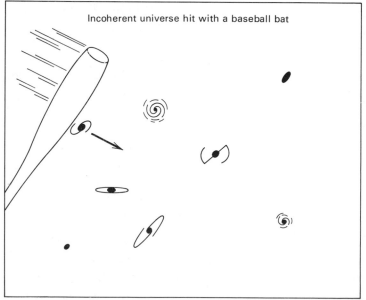

Incoherent universe hit with a baseball bat

Figure 69   Coherence.

built on a very firm and, usually, a very complicated foundation of mathematical physics and that the brief qualitative descriptions given here do not give a true idea of the nature of the theories. It is not enough in science to simply think about the universe and write down a description of some model of it. No model of the universe can be taken seriously by scientists until it has been worked out completely in mathematical and physical detail.

Newton was one of the first scientists to take what we would consider a scientific approach to the cosmological question. He attempted to apply his theory of gravitation to the entire universe, assumed to be euclidean, and he found certain difficulties in achieving this. The worst problem was that the universe, defined by the space containing matter, must be infinite in extent because, if it is finite, then Newton's law of gravity would predict that it would immediately contract to a central point. It would not be a stable universe if finite in size. More recently other difficulties of Newton's cosmological model have been pointed out. One is called *Olbers' paradox*. The astronomer Olbers showed that, if the universe is infinite in extent, the sky in all directions would not be dark, but would be extremely bright, either infinitely bright or at least as bright as the average surface brightness of a star. This would mean that, in an infinite universe, all the sky would have about the brightness of the disk of the sun. In such a universe we would hardly even detect the sun and there would be no night or day. It would be too bright and too hot on the earth for life as we know it. Since this is obviously not the case, we might conclude that the universe either is not infinite or is not homogeneous. Perhaps, we might suggest, stars become scarcer or fainter at very great distances from the sun or, perhaps, large amounts of dust absorb distant starlight. Neither of these suggestions is attractive to the cosmologist because they necessitate assuming that the sun is in a very special, or preferred, location in the universe. Many lessons have taught us that making the egotistical assumption that we are at the center of the universe is a dangerous presumption.

Another point concerning Newton's cosmology is that it and subsequent newtonian models dealt with only static (not-moving) universes and did not take into account the fact that the universe is expanding. The expansion of the universe was not known, of course, in Newton's time; so he could not take it into account. But we now know that if the universe is not static and if it does expand as we know it to do, then Olbers' paradox can be avoided. At very great distances the galaxies will be moving at such high velocities that most of their radiation will not reach us; therefore we will not expect a bright sky due to them. However, even when Newton's cosmologies are revised to take into account the expanding nature of the universe, the results are not entirely satisfactory because they cannot account for the long-established effects of relativity.

In 1917 Einstein attempted to work out his first cosmological model based on general relativity. The red shifts of the galaxies were still not known; so he assumed a static universe, without expansion. He found that the universe could not be infinite in extent, as Newton had found, nor could it be finite in extent and be surrounded by an empty infinite universe. Therefore, he suggested that space is not euclidean in nature but is finite and positively curved. When he worked out the details of the mathematics he found that, if his ideas were correct, then the radius of the curved finite space could immediately be found from the density of the universe. Astronomers have attempted to measure the density of the universe by measuring masses of galaxies and by counting galaxies and measuring their distances. From the best estimate we have today of the density of the universe, the radius calculated by using Einstein's equations would turn out to be about 3×10^{10} light years.

After the discovery of the expansion of the universe, Einstein and many others subsequently attempted to develop a relativistic cosmological model that expanded. The most general type of expanding relativistic models of the universe differ primarily in their curvature; so if the assumptions underlying them are truly correct, the main thing that observations need determine is the geometry of the universe. Generally speaking, most cosmologists today believe that one of these expanding general relativistic models is probably correct and that the curvature of the universe is the chief unknown quantity.

However, there are some doubts about the initial assumptions, outlined in the beginning of this chapter, and several recent models have been proposed which reject, for instance, the assumption of isotropy. In these models, for example, the universe might be rotating and expanding. Complications like this are very difficult to treat exactly, and there is not complete agreement among cosmologists

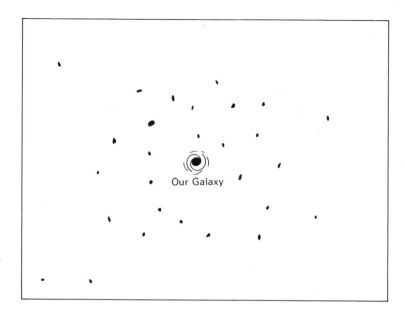

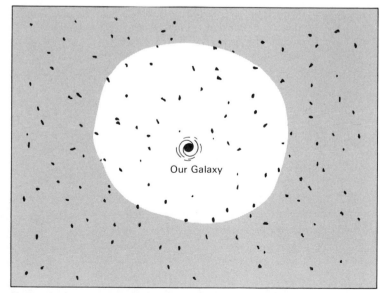

Figure 70   Two ways to avoid Olbers' paradox.

about the implications of properties such as the possible rotation of the universe.

A very different idea was proposed about 20 years ago by Bondi and Gold, who rejected the entire approach taken by their predecessors in cosmology. They hypothesized that an overriding principle should take precedence over all other principles of physics, and they called this the *perfect cosmological principle.* It leads to the conclusion that the universe and its large-scale nature are exactly the same everywhere *and at all times.* The implications of the perfect cosmological principle lead to the model of the universe called the *steady-state cosmology,* in which the universe is infinite in extent and age. As we know from measurements the universe expands; in order that its density not change as it expands, Bondi and Gold, and later Hoyle, proposed that matter is continuously created in the universe to fill up the space left by the expansion. This matter is created out of nothing, and, although it is created on an extremely slow scale—much too sparsely for us ever to detect—many scientists object to the idea of creation out of nothing because of the way it violates physical principles involving conservation.

Figure 71   The radial-velocity answer to Olbers' paradox. The most-distant galaxies have their light red-shifted so far that we do not detect it.

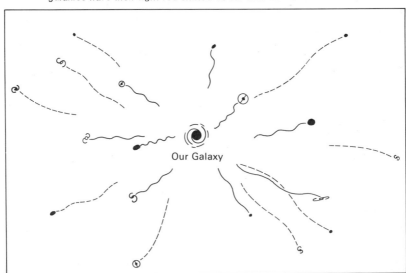

Our Galaxy

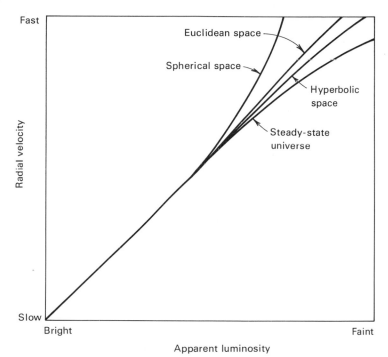

Figure 72 When the radial velocities and the distances of very-distant galaxies can be determined independently of each other, we can find out what kind of space we live in.

In addition to the steady-state model, there have been many other exotic ideas which have led to models of the universe. For instance, some scientists have suggested that the red shift of galaxies is not a doppler shift and that the universe is not truly expanding. These scientists have had to hypothesize some completely new and unspecified effect which mimics the doppler shift, and the lack of any confirmation of such an effect makes it difficult to accept this type of cosmology without considerable reservation. Other scientists have suggested that the universe might be decipherable by looking more closely at the various constants of physics and by exploring the nature of the nucleus and the atom. It is found, for instance, that certain fundamental properties of elementary particles, like the electron and the proton, can be related in a way that suggests a close

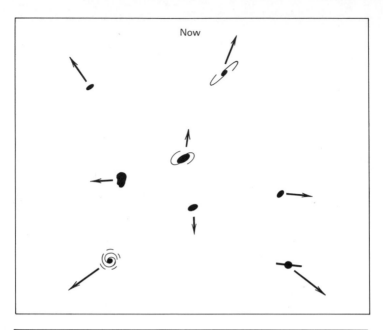

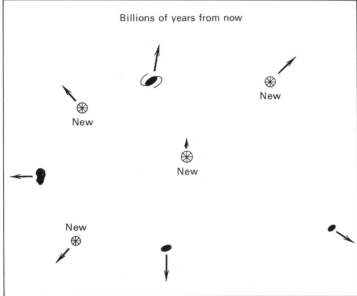

Figure 73 The steady-state universe, though expanding, always has the same density of galaxies because new galaxies are formed out of nothing.

numerical relationship with the properties of the universe as a whole. Although such juggling with physical parameters is very suggestive, its significance is not generally understood or agreed upon.

Perhaps the most important discovery in cosmology in recent years is the so-called background radiation at radio wavelengths. This has been shown to be, very probably, radiation that is "left over" from a time when the universe was very small and very hot, billions of years ago. The background radiation can best be explained as greatly red-shifted light rays produced primarily only a few hours after the universe began (the "big bang") and now so far away, so diffuse, and so rapidly receding that we can see them only at radio wavelengths. If this interpretation is correct, then the steady-state theory is impossible, and we can hope to learn a great deal about the events near the time of the beginning.

In spite of a great deal of effort on the part of astronomers to check all these different cosmological models, it is still true that we do not know which is correct, if any. It is very obvious that the problem is one of the most difficult in all science and that it will be many years before it is solved.

CHAPTER 5

THE
UNIVERSE
OF GALAXIES

The astronomer Hubble was the first to organize galaxies into a scheme where they were grouped according to appearance. Although not an evolutionary scheme, Hubble's classification of galaxies has helped immensely in our understanding of the evolution of galaxies. Hubble divided galaxies into three main types: elliptical galaxies, spiral galaxies, and irregular galaxies.

Elliptical galaxies are perfectly elliptical—their outlines are very smooth and quite perfect in this geometrical property. If we should plot a contour map of an elliptical galaxy, we would have a group of concentric ellipses with the brightest contour right in the center and increasingly faint contours outward. All these ellipses, if we measured them extremely accurately, would turn out to have exactly the same shape, just a different size. Now what does this suggest? These are very smoothly organized systems of stars, and the fact that there is no structure except this smooth, perfect structure suggests they might be very old, undisturbed galaxies—galaxies in which nothing has happened for a long long time. Measures of ages of elliptical galaxies confirm this suspicion. Also, if we look at how the light is distributed from the center outward, we find that the intensity decreases outward in a nice, smooth, curved line. The remarkable thing is that the curve describing this structure for *all* elliptical galaxies is the *same*, except for the scale and the degree of

Figure 74   An elliptical galaxy (NGC 3377).

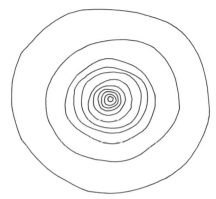

Figure 75 A contour map of an elliptical galaxy (NGC 3379), showing lines of equal brightness.

flatness. There is a formula that describes all elliptical galaxies—they all have the same basic structure, except for two scale factors, one being related to how rich the whole thing is and the other telling how wide this distribution is. This fact turns out to be extremely important since it indicates that the systems are in, what is called in physics, a *relaxed state,* meaning that it has been a long time since the system was formed, long enough, in fact, that there is absolutely no trace left of the initial conditions. Like a bag of potato chips left unopened in the back seat of the car for several months, the original shape of a relaxed galaxy has been completely erased by its intervening history and experiences.

One can calculate how long it takes for an elliptical galaxy to become relaxed. It depends on the size and compactness of the elliptical galaxy. Calculations show that it takes a very long time, on the order of a billion years, in some cases much longer, for an elliptical galaxy to relax. So the evidence that these elliptical galaxies are relaxed indicates they are very old indeed.

The elliptical galaxies are usually made up of billions of stars, all of which have orbits around the center of mass of the system. By comparing the structure of these galaxies with that of theoretical, mathematically constructed models, we can actually determine what kinds of orbits such a system has. Different galaxies have different arrangements of orbits, but most of the elliptical galaxies have a

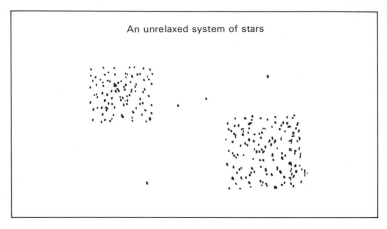

An unrelaxed system of stars

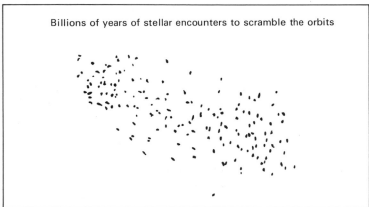

Billions of years of stellar encounters to scramble the orbits

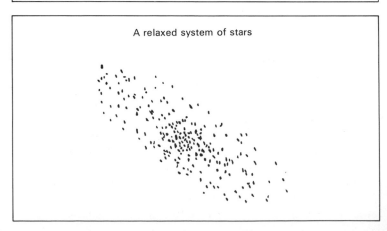

A relaxed system of stars

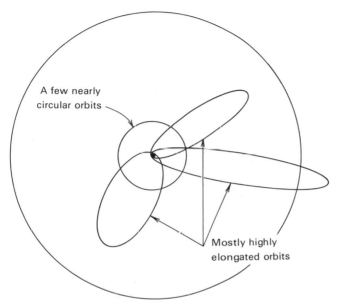

A few nearly
circular orbits

Mostly highly
elongated orbits

Figure 77   Samples of orbits of stars in an elliptical galaxy.

large percentage of stars with extremely eccentric orbits. The
earth's orbit around the sun is nearly circular; yet, in the case of most
of the stars in most elliptical galaxies, orbits are *not* circular at all
but are very elongated. There are always a few stars that have
nearly circular orbits, and the different elliptical galaxies have different percentages of highly elongated and circular orbits.

   Another important uniformity for elliptical galaxies is their color.
All elliptical galaxies are red, and there is very little variation in
color from one to another. There is some difference, and this is important, but it is only important because we don't understand why
there is any small amount of variation at all. The most significant
thing is that all elliptical galaxies are red, and we find that this can
be true only if the elliptical galaxies consist primarily of old stars.
Studies of stars in our Galaxy show that young stars are blue, and
you can't have a red galaxy made up of blue stars. The elliptical gal-

Figure 76   Relaxation.

axies must be made up of old stars, a fact that we have already deduced above from other evidence.

The spectra of galaxies are further rich sources of information. When we look at the spectrum of an elliptical galaxy, we are looking at a superposition of all the spectra of stars in the system, and we get a sort of average spectrum, giving a good general idea of what kind of stars are there. Spectra also indicate that the stars in elliptical galaxies are old. No young stars show up in the spectra.

A further uniform property of elliptical galaxies is that they contain only stars but nothing else we can detect—no gas clouds or dust clouds (with very infrequent and minor exceptions). This implies that there cannot be any stars forming now in elliptical galaxies because a star has to form out of something, and we know that stars form, in fact, out of gas and dust. If there are no raw materials, stars cannot be built. The condensation of gas and dust to form stars is always spectacular in that it always happens in the midst of huge, glowing, turbulent clouds of material. No such gas and dust means that nothing much has been going on in elliptical galaxies nor will go on in them for a very long time. They are very staid and stable objects.

In the Hubble classification, elliptical galaxies are divided into eight groups, depending on their appearance. This is not a physical distinction, just a geometrical one. Some elliptical galaxies are nearly circular in outline, whereas others are highly elongated. The eccentricity of an ellipse is a measure of how stretched it is, and that, of course, is a measure of the ratio of the minor to the major axis of the system. If we call the major axis a and the minor axis b, then the Hubble subclasses are defined according to the following scheme: first assign an E, meaning elliptical, then follow it by a number N, where N is equal to $10 \times (a - b) / a$. For a galaxy with a circular outline, where a and b are equal, N is 0, so the galaxy is called an E0. For a highly eccentric ellipse, for instance, one with b that is three-tenths of a, the classification would be E7. We have eight classes, E0 through E7. Hubble found no galaxies flatter than E7 among the elliptical galaxies—they just do not exist; so we stop at E7.

The second type of galaxy is the spiral galaxy. This is the kind that we usually think of when we think of galaxies. They are usually beautiful and spectacular objects. Spiral galaxies are very flat, ex-

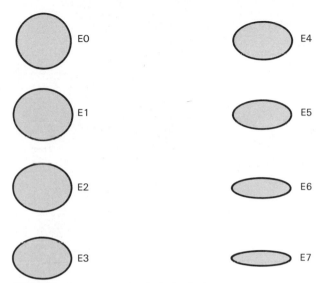

Figure 78   Subclasses of elliptical galaxies.

cept for the central regions, a fact that can be deduced from the statistics of the orientation of spirals as seen in the sky. Enough of them are seen that are very very thin to infer from this distribution that most of them are extremely flat, with an average value of 0.8 for the quantity $(a - b)/a$. If they were elliptical galaxies (which of course they are not) one would call them E8. What does their flatness tell us? One way that we can get something to be flat is to make it rotate. Galaxies that rotate fast should be flat, especially gas-rich galaxies, all the material of which has not yet condensed into stars.

Using the doppler shift, we have actually been able to measure the rotation of some spiral galaxies. This turns out to corroborate what might be suspected from the fact that they are flat. They do rotate, some very rapidly. The rotation, however, is not like that of a solid body, such as the earth. Because the stars and gas clouds are not held together rigidly by anything, the speed of rotation is different at different distances from the center. In the outer parts they revolve like the planets do around the sun—the more distant ones moving more slowly. In the inner regions the stars revolve at

Figure 79 A spiral galaxy with a peculiar companion (NGC 5194 and 5195).

Figure 80 A photograph of a nearly edge-on spiral galaxy showing how flat it is.

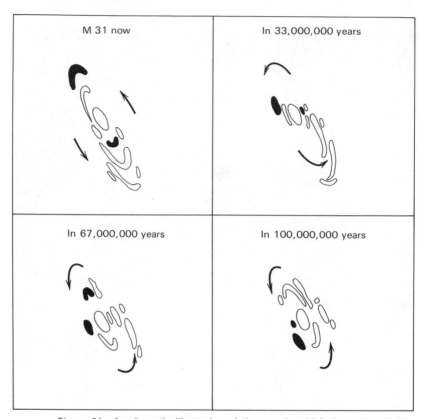

Figure 81 A schematic illustration of the way in which the galaxy M 31, shown in Figure 14, will rotate between now and 100,000,000 years from now. Bright segments of spiral arms are delineated. Two are blacked in to make it easy to follow them around.

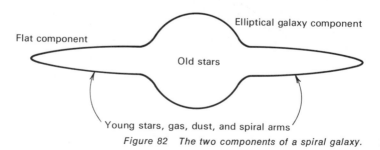

Figure 82 The two components of a spiral galaxy.

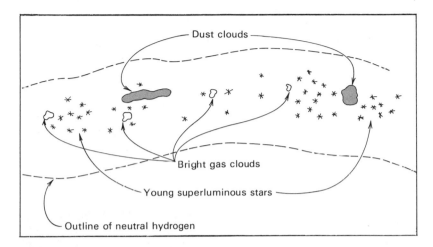

Figure 83   Four components of spiral arms.

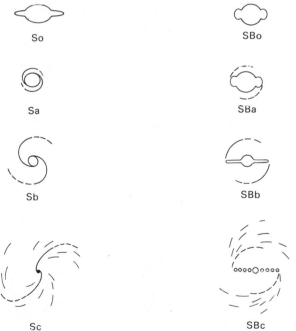

So

SBo

Sa

SBa

Sb

SBb

Sc

SBc

Figure 84   Subclasses of spiral galaxies.

about the same speed, more like a solid body, because the gravitational pull that causes them to revolve is not just in the center of the galaxy but is all around them.

It has been found that spiral galaxies can be thought of as having two components in their structure, an elliptical component and a flat component. Spiral galaxies seem to have superimposed themselves on elliptical galaxies. The central parts have structures like those of elliptical galaxies, and, added to that, there is a flat distribution of stars having a very different structure. The elliptical component has elliptical contours, old stars, no gas, no dust, and it follows the law of elliptical-galaxy structure. The flat component, however, is very

Figure 85   An S0 galaxy (NGC 1332).

nonuniform. It is the part that contains the most spectacular feature of this type of galaxy, the spiral arms. Most spiral galaxies contain two spiral arms, and sometimes these are highly branched. In some galaxies the spiral arms are very open and in other galaxies they are very tightly closed. The reason the spiral arms show up at all is that they are unusual in their makeup. They contain something other than just old stars; in fact, they contain three things that are highly conspicuous: very young stars, gas, and dust. The gas shows up in two forms: first as giant gas clouds that can be seen glowing brightly; second as invisible (except to radio telescopes) neutral hydrogen clouds that extend over the entire arm structure. Dust shows up very

Figure 86   An Sc galaxy (NGC 5457).

Figure 87   An SBb galaxy (NGC 4303).

conspicuously as dark blobs of matter that obscure the stars behind them. The young stars show up very clearly, at least in the nearer spiral galaxies, as being very bright very blue stars. From this evidence there is one thing that we can deduce about the arms: they are the locus of star formation in the galaxies. We know that is where stars are being formed because we find stars there as young as only 1 million years, or less, which is very young considering that these galaxies are 10 billion years old altogether. And we find the raw materials, gas and dust, in clouds, ready to make stars in the future; so star formation is going on in these arms and will continue to do so.

Why do the arms exist? Nobody knows. This is one of astronomy's very intriguing unanswered questions. There are many ideas, but none of them has been proved beyond doubt to be correct as yet. They may be due to pressure waves in the gas or to magnetic fields; magnetic fields exist in galaxies on a very large scale, and they tend to line up along spiral arms.

Hubble divided the spiral galaxies into eight different subclasses. First are the S0 spirals, which have everything except the spiral structure. The characteristics we have listed for spiral galaxies exist as far as structure is concerned—they have the flat component and the elliptical component but they have no spiral arms. Some of them

Figure 88   An irregular galaxy, the Large Magellanic Cloud.

have dust, some have a little gas, but none of them have real spiral arms.

The next four subclasses are defined according to how tightly wound the arms are. An Sa spiral has really tight arms, an Sb has less tight arms, whereas those of an Sc are very loose and spread out. Hubble also showed that there was an anomalous feature among a few spirals: instead of having a simple nucleus that looks like an elliptical galaxy, some have this nucleus plus a "bar." The bar is a very strange long, narrow structure, bright and straight and centered on the nucleus, and it is from the ends of the bar that the

Figure 89   A peculiar galaxy with an elliptical-like nucleus and segments of spiral arms on only one side (NGC 5474).

arms usually emanate. Hubble distinguished these objects by insert-
ing a B between the S and the 0, a, b, or c. Otherwise, the subclasses are similarly defined. A barred spiral without arms is an SB0,
one with tight arms is an SBa, and so on down the sequence. The bar
of a barred spiral is still very much an enigma. We do not know why
or how it can exist, and a great deal of current research is going into
solving this puzzle.

The third main type of galaxy is the "irregular" class. Generally,
irregular galaxies have the same stellar make-up as spiral galaxies,
but without well-defined spiral arms. They sometimes have bars,

Figure 90   A peculiar irregular galaxy (NGC 3077).

seldom have a clearly identifiable nucleus, and always contain large amounts of young stars, gas, and dust. Often an irregular galaxy also contains many star clusters, many more than a spiral of the same total population would have. The outstanding character of a typical irregular galaxy is *youth*. Although all such galaxies also appear to contain some old stars, most of the light from an irregular galaxy comes from its abundant and brilliant young stars and its luminous gas clouds. Irregular galaxies rotate, like spiral galaxies, but, for reasons which we do not yet know, spiral arms do not form. It is true, however, that some irregular galaxies have what look like "primitive," distorted, or partly formed spiral arms, and there thus seems to be a transition from the Sc galaxies to the irregular ones.

Not quite all galaxies fit into Hubble's simple classification scheme, and most of the odd ones are very odd indeed. We now have reason to believe that certain galaxies are experiencing huge violent, disruptive, and explosive events, the result being an unclassifiable mess of stars, gas and dust. The next chapter discusses these explosive galaxies in detail.

CHAPTER 6

GALAXIES IN EXPLOSION

Among the most exciting and bewildering objects in the universe are the galaxies that seem to be in the process of explosion. We do not yet know why these galaxies are experiencing violence, but we are continually gaining more evidence on the nature of the violent events. The most remarkable feature of these explosions is their size. An explosion that can disrupt an entire galaxy, made up of a million million stars, is an immense explosion indeed.

Explosions in galaxies were first detected by radio telescopes. Whereas ordinary galaxies normally emit most of their radiation in the form of normal light, it was discovered many years ago that some peculiar-looking galaxies also emit radio radiation. Over the last few years detailed studies of these strange objects, using *both* radio telescopes and large optical telescopes, have shown that the only reasonable explanation of the source of radio emission is some type of explosion of matter.

How big are these explosions? In physics and astronomy an energetic event like an explosion is usually measured in terms of the amount of energy released. The unit used in most cases is called the *erg*. An erg is a very small unit of energy, and energy is the capacity to do work. When an average person climbs up one stair of a staircase, this work amounts to 1 billion (10^9) ergs. One ton of TNT, when exploded, releases 4×10^{16} ergs of energy, whereas a 20-kiloton

1 erg

A beetle climbing onto a piece of cardboard

1 billion ergs

A man climbing up one step

Figure 91   1 erg and 1 billion ergs.

atomic bomb gives off 10^{21} ergs. A major volcanic eruption can give off energy equivalent to many atomic bombs.

We can measure, for example, for an erupting volcano, both the rate of release of energy (in ergs per second) and the total energy given off over the entire time of the eruption. For instance, the rate of energy release from the eruption of Surtsey, the volcano that recently formed a new island off the coast of Iceland, averaged about 10^{18} ergs per second. The eruption lasted for months, so that the total energy given off was about 10^{25} ergs!

Even more energy is released in some of the types of explosive events that we have witnessed among the stars. The least energetic of these is immensely more powerful than the biggest volcanic eruption witnessed on the earth. These are the so-called solar flares, which occur from time to time on the gaseous surface of the sun. They eject vast numbers of nuclear particles from the sun, some of which reach the earth, causing the northern lights (and, of course,

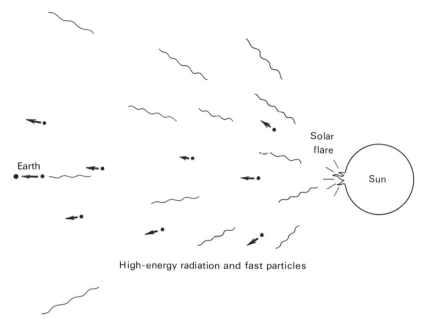

Figure 92   A solar flare can influence the earth's outer atmosphere.

the southern lights). The particles emitted by the explosive solar flares also greatly disturb the Van Allen belts, the famous radiation belts that surround the earth and that were discovered by the earliest artificial satellites. Solar flares are of further current interest because of their possible danger to astronauts making long space flights to the moon or to the nearest planets. The average high-intensity solar flare explodes with a total energy so large that it would take the equivalent of over a million volcanoes to equal it, averaging some 10^{31} ergs total.

A much more energetic explosion of stellar material is that of a nova. Stars, when they reach a certain period in their evolution, experience a particular type of instability that, in some cases, leads to a tremendous violent explosion of material from the outer parts of the star. This produces what is called a *nova,* so named because it brightens so fast and so much that it appears to be a "new" star. The energy of the explosion is so great that the star experiencing it becomes thousands of times brighter than normal, and thus appears briefly as a new star. An ordinary nova explosion is about 100 million million times as powerful as a solar flare. This means a total energy of 10^{44} ergs.

Even more explosive than a nova is an object that becomes so luminous it is called a *supernova*. Supernovae are extremely rare objects, so rare that they occur only about once in every 100 to 300 years in each galaxy. From what we find by studying the remains of a supernova explosion, it appears that, when a supernova "goes off," the entire star is destroyed by the explosion. This is an extremely impressive demolition job, and when it occurs, all the gaseous ma-

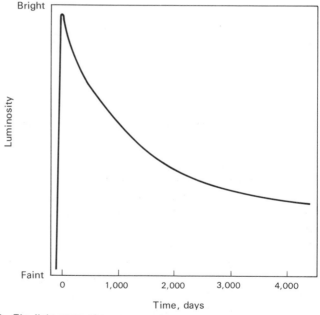

Figure 93   The light curve of a nova.

Figure 94   A supernova in a spiral galaxy (NGC 4303). The photograph at the bottom was taken in 1961, shortly after the supernova outburst; the photograph at the top was taken four years later, after the supernova had faded from view.

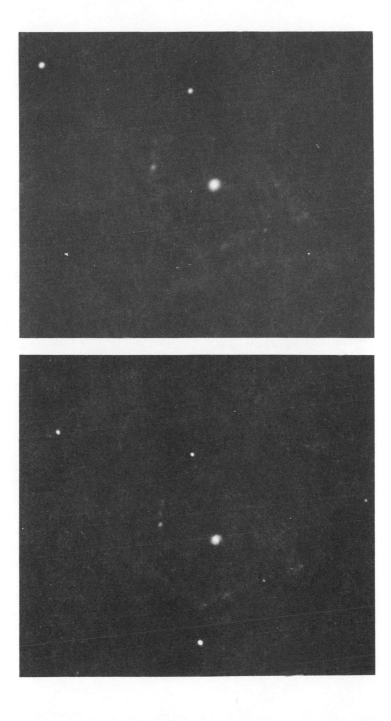

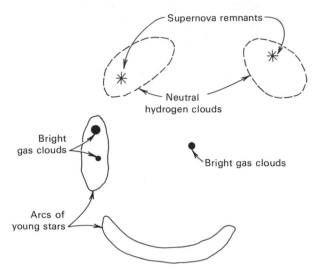

Figure 95   *The remnants of a supersupernova tentatively identified in a nearby galaxy (the LMC). The explosion pushed the gas in the galaxy back into arcs to make the observed arcs of young stars and gas clouds, which contain supernova remnants and bright gas clouds.*

terial that made up the star is thrown out into the space around it in the form of an immense rapidly expanding cloud. These clouds become strong sources of radio emission and can be detected by radio telescopes. The reason radio emission comes from these clouds is that they consist partly of nuclear particles, electrons and protons, traveling so fast they are almost going the speed of light, and they are traveling through magnetic fields. It is well known in physics that, when charged particles like this travel at high velocity along magnetic fields, they emit a certain kind of radiation, called *synchrotron radiation,* that is strong at radio wavelengths (between 1 centimeter and 100 meters). On the average, the amount of energy produced in a supernova explosion is about 10,000 times that of a nova explosion. In ergs this energy totals up to 10^{49} ergs.

Even more energetic than the supernova is a very recently discovered phenomenon called the *supersupernova.* We know at the time of this writing of only a few such explosions, all of which occurred perhaps millions of years ago and for which we see only the

Figure 96   An exploding galaxy (M 87). This short-exposure photograph shows the nucleus of the galaxy and a jet of exploding material apparently emanating from the nucleus.

circumstantial evidence made up of remnants. Nevertheless, from the evidence that remains, it is possible to learn that supersupernova explosions, whatever their cause, are so energetic they throw out vast amounts of material, the equivalent, perhaps, of a million suns. They can completely disrupt portions of galaxies. The estimate of the energy in a supersupernova explosion is approximately 1 million times that of an ordinary supernova. In ergs this energy is 10^{54} ergs.

We have seen that, although they are rare, we know of explosive events almost big enough to disrupt whole galaxies. The range of energies of the explosions we have described is immense, and this range is considerably extended when we look at the total energies involved in the explosive galaxies. Typically the total amount of energy involved in the *most* energetic radio galaxies is about 10 million times that of a supersupernova. Explosive galaxies *average* approximately 10^{58} ergs, the equivalent of thousands of supersupernovae.

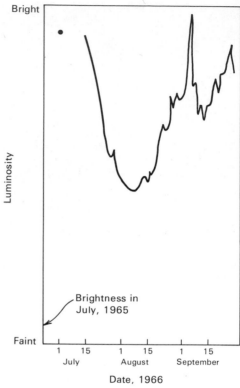

Figure 97   *Light curve of a quasar (3C 446) as measured in the summer of 1966.*

In general, the explosive objects we can identify as extragalactic (beyond the edges of our Galaxy, the Milky Way) can be divided into two classes: first are the quasi-stellar objects, which include the quasars and the quasi-stellar blue objects; second are the radio galaxies. The quasars are those weird and, as yet, unexplained objects that emit very intense radio emission and that look optically very much like stars. Since their discovery in 1961, there has been no end to the controversy and confusion they have produced. Here are some of their characteristics: they have a very small apparent size, both in optical photographs and according to radio-telescopic

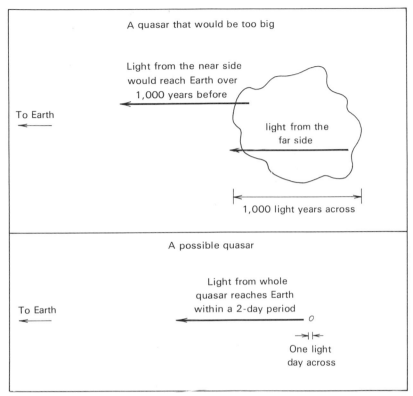

Figure 98   Why a quasar must be small if we see it change in brightness within a day or two.

measurements. They appear very much smaller than known galaxies and most would not be distinguishable from stars by ordinary techniques. They have very broad emission lines in their spectra, telling that they are made up of extremely hot gas with large turbulent velocities. Their radial velocities, as measured from the doppler shifts in their emission lines, are very very large, ranging from several thousand miles per second up to velocities of about 80 percent the velocity of light. They sometimes show rapid and usually irregular fluctuations in their intensities over a few days or a few weeks, and these fluctuations in intensity immediately tell us that the objects are intrinsically very small. If they were many light years across, the whole object could not vary in luminosity over a short period because of the light-travel time from one side to the other. If, for instance, an object 1,000 light years across is acting like a quasar, and, if it suddenly changed in brightness all over in some mysterious synchronous way, then we would see this occur first at the nearest part of the galaxy and then, 1,000 years from now, we would see this variation occur at the farthest part. The entire variation would be spread over a period of 1,000 years as seen by us. Therefore, it is argued, we cannot, in the case of quasars, be looking at objects that are more than a few light days across. And yet the quasars are so bright and so energetic at both visual and radio wavelengths that it is almost impossible to imagine so much going on in such a very small object. Some astronomers have argued that the quasars are not as distant as their red shifts would indicate, and this may someday be proven to be the case; but at the time of the writing of this chapter we have nothing to support such an idea. We are left with conflicting evidence. Quasars are either much too close for their red shifts, or they are much too energetic for their size.

The other type of extragalactic explosive object is the so-called normal radio galaxy. These show very strong emission at radio wavelengths, but otherwise look like ordinary galaxies, though with certain optically evident peculiarities. In general, most of the radio galaxies that have been identified with optical objects appear to be somewhat disrupted things that show bright emission of light from the nucleus and often show vast quantities of dust and gas strewn about in a chaotic manner. In some cases the image appears to be that of an ordinary elliptical galaxy, but with a chaotic or unusual arrangement of dust and gas superimposed on it.

The total amount of energy involved in the type of explosion that causes radio galaxies and quasars is so big that it would be necessary, to produce this energy by ordinary nuclear reactions, to completely annihilate billions of suns. How can such an explosion occur? What actually causes it, and what is the means by which all this energy is released? There have been many suggestions of explanations proposed over the last few years, and in the next paragraphs we review these theories to see whether any of them can explain all of the details about quasars and radio galaxies.

When radio galaxies were first discovered, it was believed that the cause of the disruption as well as the high rate of emission of energy was the collision of two galaxies. Galaxies probably do collide occasionally, and it was hypothesized that when such collisions occur a very disruptive and energetic event results. In fact, however, we know the stars in galaxies are spread out so thinly and the sizes of the stars are so small compared to their distances apart that two galaxies made up only of stars would pass cleanly through each other without any violent collision occurring. The stars would merely appear for a while to be twice too numerous to an observer in such a colliding galaxy, and then they would thin out again to their normal

Figure 99   M 82, a galaxy that exploded only a few million years ago.

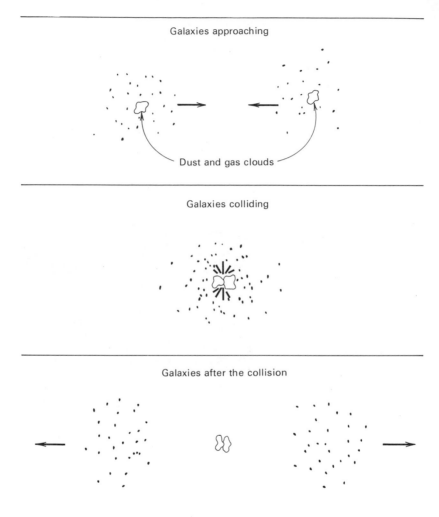

Galaxies approaching

Dust and gas clouds

Galaxies colliding

Galaxies after the collision

Figure 100   *Two galaxies that collide leave behind their clouds of gas and dust, but their stars do not collide.*

density as the two galaxies neatly passed through each other. The probability that even one star of one galaxy would collide with one star of another galaxy during such a collision of galaxies is small. However, if such a colliding galaxy contains gas and dust clouds that are very large compared to the sizes of stars, then there would occur a very violent collision. Unfortunately for this idea, the amount of energy produced by such a collision of gas and dust clouds in galaxies is not large enough to explain the most energetic radio sources, and, even worse, none of the nearby radio galaxies turn out to be cases of galaxies in collision. They are apparently only single objects, and we find by measuring their radial velocities and by making detailed studies of their structure that the collision hypothesis simply does not apply.

Another early theory suggested to explain the high energy output from radio sources is that they represent an encounter of matter with antimatter. We know from physics that there is a fairly strict symmetry in nature between two different forms of material, one of which we call *ordinary matter*—the kind of material that we, our earth, the sun, and everything that we come in contact with is known to be made up of—and the other *antimatter*—which looks the same except that it is exactly opposite in charge and in other fundamental properties, thus having the property of annihilation when it comes in contact with matter. For instance, the proton is an ordinary elementary particle of matter. Several years ago it was found that there is another particle with the same mass as the proton but with negative instead of positive charge; this was called the *antiproton*. Experimentally it was found that a proton and an antiproton, when brought together, annihilate each other and produce energy in their place. Although there is no evidence that antimatter exists in nature (we have always had to produce it in the laboratory), there is still the idea that, perhaps, elsewhere in the universe there are galaxies made up of stars of antimatter. If one of those galaxies should collide with one of the galaxies of matter, it has been suggested, perhaps a quasar or extremely strong radio galaxy might result. At present this theory is not held by very many people because of the difficulties involved in understanding why such a collision would proceed for very long. One can show that, as soon as two clouds of gas, one made up of matter and the other made up of antimatter, should come close to each other, the first few atoms that would col-

Galaxies approaching

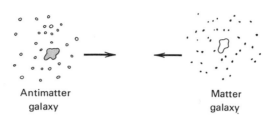

Antimatter
galaxy

Matter
galaxy

Galaxies colliding

Galaxies after the collision

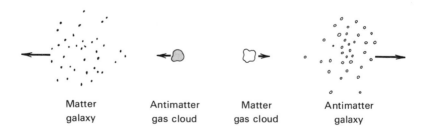

Matter
galaxy

Antimatter
gas cloud

Matter
gas cloud

Antimatter
galaxy

Figure 101   The collision of a galaxy of antimatter with a galaxy of matter.

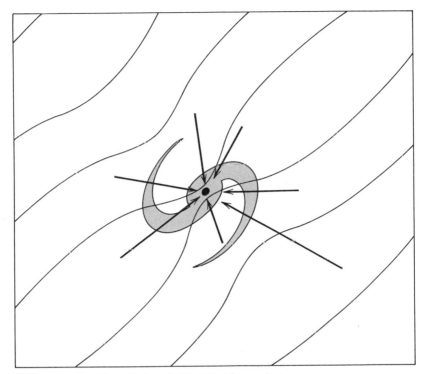

Figure 102   Accretion of intergalactic matter by a galaxy.

lide and annihilate each other would cause a heating up of that portion of the collision edge of the two clouds to the point where the two
clouds would then separate and no large collision would ever result.

Another idea put forward to explain radio sources is that of accretion of matter. It was suggested that large amounts of matter between the galaxies might fall into a galaxy under the galaxy's gravitational pull, and the nucleus of the galaxy would eventually experience a tremendous overpopulation of matter, which would cause an
explosion. In detail, however, it is calculated that the amount of ex-
isting intergalactic matter is not sufficiently large to explain an explosion as large as we observe.

A fourth idea suggested to explain these strange objects is that
these galaxies are being observed in the process of formation. This

idea was particularly suggested for the quasars. One of the biggest difficulties in explaining quasars in terms of the formation of galaxies is the difficulty of size. We find that a galaxy forming out of a large cloud of intergalactic material will condense, if conditions are correct, to a small object, much smaller than when it eventually becomes a stable and well-formed galaxy, but not sufficiently small to allow the strange short-period variations that quasars exhibit.

Another idea published is that magnetic flares occur in galaxies. This phenomenon, which is well known in the case of the solar sur-

Figure 103   Formation of a galaxy with moderate rotation.

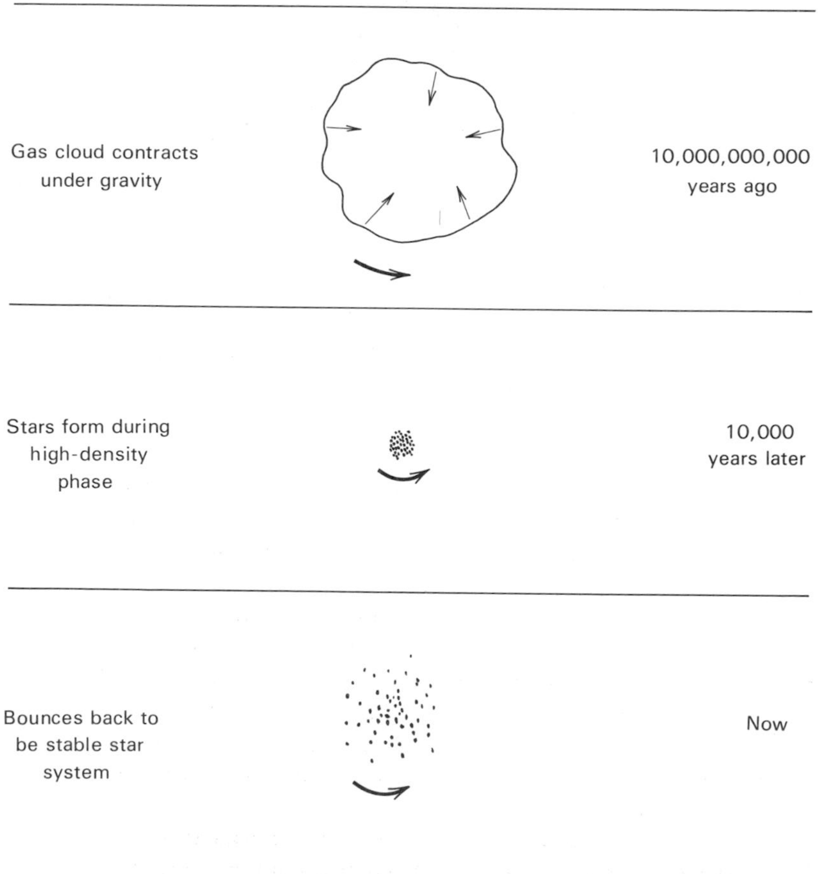

Gas cloud contracts
under gravity

10,000,000,000
years ago

Stars form during
high-density
phase

10,000
years later

Bounces back to
be stable star
system

Now

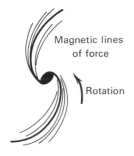

Magnetic lines
of force

Rotation

Magnetic lines
of force wound
up tightly into
nucleus

BANG

Magnetic
discharge

Figure 104   A magnetic flare.

face, where magnetic fields are whipped about because of motions of charged particles in the sun's atmosphere, might also occur in galaxies. Perhaps the spiral arms have magnetic fields imbedded in them, as some evidence suggests, and, if spiral arms wind up as the galaxy rotates, these magnetic fields might become compressed to the center until they discharge. This would be roughly analogous to the way lightning discharges when too much electricity accumulates in the atmosphere of the earth. However, it has been found that the amount of energy required to explain quasars and radio galaxies is just too much to be explained by magnetic flares, assuming what we believe are reasonable ideas regarding the strength of magnetic fields in galaxies.

Yet another idea suggested is that these objects may be exhibiting supernova explosions which occur so frequently they start a chain reaction. The idea here is that, in the centers of the nuclei of galaxies, objects which might become supernovae are packed together so tightly that when one goes off as a supernova, exploding, it triggers all the other stars near it so that they also go off, each of them triggering several more, so that a chain reaction of supernovae results. This sort of event could produce a great deal of energy, but probably not enough to explain the most energetic of the radio sources. It also fails to provide a reasonable mechanism whereby one supernova can cause another to explode. This last argument is not terribly strong because we do not know for sure what causes a supernova to explode in the first place, although it certainly appears to be concerned with the instability of the center of the star during

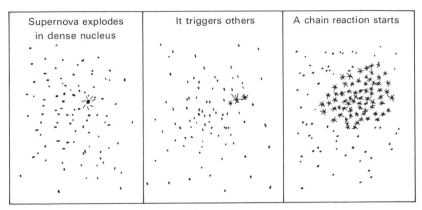

| Supernova explodes in dense nucleus | It triggers others | A chain reaction starts |

Figure 105   A supernova chain reaction.

its later stages of evolution, and there is no easy way in which an external effect, such as the explosion of a nearby supernova, might trigger such an instability.

One final idea we might consider is that of a gravitational collapse. There has been a suggestion that, if a very large and massive object should collapse under its own gravity, gravitational energy could be released in sufficient quantity to explain the radio sources, particularly the quasars. It is possible that this hypothesis may work, but in nature there are difficulties in finding the appropriate

Figure 106   Gravitational collapse of a supermassive object.

A supermassive object collapses under gravity

Gravitational energy is released as radiation

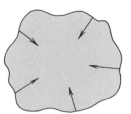

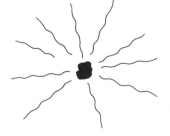

object to collapse and in finding a means by which a sufficient quantity of gravitational energy can be released from an object as small as quasars seem to be.

As the above theories have shown, astronomers and physicists have been spending a great deal of time and thought in attempting to explain galaxies that seem to be in the process of explosion. But it cannot be said at this time that we have succeeded in explaining these strange objects because none of the theories is fully satisfactory. More needs to be known about their characteristics, their distances, and their mechanisms whereby energy is released. Hopefully, when such knowledge is attained, we can find out what immense forces are at work when an entire galaxy is disrupted or blown apart.

Have we stumbled onto a new law of physics, or a new physical force, more powerful than any now known? Are we observing some strange coincidence or juxtaposition of events too rare to be expected from our knowledge of the local universe? Or are we being misled in our interpretation of the features of these objects by some subtly incorrect deduction? We do not know the answer, but we do know that the universe is full of surprises, and we certainly have not seen the end of them.

INDEX

INDEX

This book was set in Helvetica, printed on permanent paper and bound by Vail-Ballou Press, Inc. The designer was Paula E. Tuerk; the drawings were done by B. Handelman Associates, Inc. The editors were Bradford Bayne and James W. Dradley. Robert R. Laffler supervised the production.